THE
CLASSIC
HUNDRED

The Top 500 Poems
William Harmon, ed. (1992)

The Columbia Granger's® Dictionary of Poetry Quotations
Edith P. Hazen, ed. (1992)

The Columbia Granger's® World of Poetry CD-ROM (1991)

The Columbia Granger's® Index to Poetry, Ninth Edition,
Edith P. Hazen and Deborah J. Fryer, eds. (1990)

The Columbia Granger's® Guide to Poetry Anthologies.
William Katz and Linda Sternberg Katz, eds. (1990)

The Columbia Literary History of the United States
Emory Elliott, ed. (1988)

The Columbia History of the American Novel
Emory Elliott, ed. (1991)

The Concise Columbia Dictionary of Quotations.
Robert Andrews, ed. (1989)

The Concise Columbia Encyclopedia, Second Edition (1989)

THE
CLASSIC
HUNDRED

All-Time Favorite Poems

Edited by

WILLIAM HARMON

COLUMBIA

UNIVERSITY

PRESS

NEW YORK

Columbia University Press thanks its friend,
Corliss Lamont, for his gift toward the costs of
publishing this book.

COLUMBIA UNIVERSITY PRESS
NEW YORK   OXFORD

Library of Congress Cataloging-in-Publication Data
The Classic Hundred / edited by William Harmon.
    p. cm.
Includes indexes.
ISBN 0-231-08238-X (acid-free paper) (cl.)
ISBN 0-231-08239-8 (pbk.)
    1. English poetry. 2. American poetry. I. Harmon,
William, 1938-   . II. Title: All-Time Favorite Poems
821.008—dc20   92-32699   CIP

Pages 243-44 constitute an extension of
this copyright page.

This book was first published
in 1990 under the title
*The Concise Columbia
Book of Poetry.*

Clothbound editions of
Columbia University Press books
are Smyth-sewn and printed
on permanent and durable
acid-free paper.

Printed in the United States of America

10 9 8 7

CONTENTS

THE
CLASSIC
HUNDRED

THE GREATEST HITS OF
POETRY IN ENGLISH

These are the hundred poems in English that have been most anthologized, as calculated from the ninth edition of *The Columbia Granger's®️ Index to Poetry*. It is the best available record of the poems that have achieved the greatest success for the longest time with the largest number of readers.

The successive editions of *The Columbia Granger's®️* (known for decades by librarians as *"Granger's"*) show a progressive gain in sophistication, and so, apparently, does the taste of English-speaking readers. This group of a hundred poems, unlike a comparable group based on some of the earlier editions, is something that all of us—general readers, poets, and critics alike—can be proud of. During the preparation of the book I have been looking closely at these poems—virtually *living* with them—and the experience has been accompanied, from first to last, by a sense of excitement and delight.

Each edition of *The Columbia Granger's®️* has been based on a different batch of sources, and for a while in the early years those included more than poetry anthologies. Here is what the original title page looked like:

An Index
To
Poetry and Recitations
Being a Practical
Reference Manual for the Librarian
Teacher, Bookseller,
Elocutionist
etc.
Including over Thirty Thousand Titles
from Three Hundred and Sixty-Nine Books
Edited by
Edith Granger, A. B.

That was 1904. Now, recitations are dying and elocutionists are dead, persisting only in fossilized or mummified form among Moose Lodges and suchlike establishments; we no longer list an editor's degree on a title page, nor does *The Columbia Granger's®* any longer include, in addition to anthologies proper, books by such individual authors as James Whitcomb Riley and Edgar A. Guest.

In time, the recitations dropped away and only anthologies of poetry were consulted, with the list changing somewhat from edition to edition. The ninth edition is distinguished by its recognition of many anthologies of poetry in translation, although almost none of the poems in this book could be called genuine translations: W. B. Yeats's "When You Are Old" may make it as a translation from Ronsard, but Ezra Pound's "The River-Merchant's Wife: A Letter," although certainly a brilliant and beautiful poem in its own right, is a far cry from counting as a true translation from Li Po.

There may be some questions about certain poets who are not included among the finalists in this collection, and I can picture a headline:

WHERE ARE CHAUCER, POPE, BURNS, AND WHITMAN?

It may be that Chaucer and Burns wrote in a language or dialect a little too far from Modern English; a recent New Year's Eve feature on television established that most Americans don't know what they're saying when they sing "Auld Lang Syne." Pope and Whitman (and Dryden and Longfellow, for that matter) specialized in a sort of poem different from the short, independent, compassable verses that are most often and most easily anthologized. I count fifteen sonnets among the hundred poems here; Chaucer, Pope, and Whitman did not write sonnets. Some other celebrated poets wrote so many popular poems that different anthologies have chosen different poems; these poets lack the concentrated appeal that perforce attends the one or two famous works of Carew, Lovelace, Suckling, Dowson, Owen, and Jarrell, say, who seem to benefit from their own limitations. They were certainly less great, on the whole, than Chaucer, Dryden, Pope, or Whitman, and the result is that anthologists keep choosing the same few gems. Whitman wrote so many engaging poems that no single work is forced to stand out, shouldering the whole burden of a reputation.

For the record, we have here a hundred poems by forty-seven named and three anonymous poets. Only six of the poems come from longer works: four songs from plays by Shakespeare and Nashe, one song from a "medley" by Tennyson, and the proem of a long poem by Crane. ("Jabberwocky" appeared in a prose work but had appeared before that as a separate work.)

Eighty-six of the poems are British, fourteen American; one could expect a certain disproportion here, since British literary history—as far as the English language is concerned, at any rate—has been going on for several centuries longer.

The breakdown by period is interesting:

Before 1600	14
1600–1699	25
1700–1799	6
1800–1899 (British)	32
1800–1899 (American)	5
After 1900 (British)	8
After 1900 (American)	9

The tides of taste and fashion follow lines other than century boundaries, for some reason, and a midcentury-to-midcentury tabulation is revealing:

Before 1550	4
1551–1650	35
1651–1750	2
1751–1850 (British)	22
1751–1850 (American)	2
After 1851 (British)	23
After 1851 (American)	12

Moreover, both of the poems in the 1651–1750 group are by the same poet: Thomas Gray.

Shakespeare leads all the rest with eight poems. Donne is next with six. Four poets have five poems here: Blake, Keats, Tennyson, and Yeats. Two have four poems: Wordsworth and Hopkins. Herbert, Herrick, and Dickinson—along with Anonymous—are represented by three poems. Of the rest, thirty-six poets appear with one or two poems.

As I have said, there are fifteen sonnets among these hundred poems, as well as a "curtal sonnet" by Hopkins ("Pied Beauty"), which has fewer than fourteen lines. Twenty-nine of the poems are in a four-line (quatrain) stanza of some sort. There is one entry each for terza rima (Shelley's "Ode to the West Wind"), ottava rima (Yeats's "Sailing to Byzantium"), rhyme royal (Wyatt's "The Lover Showeth How He Is Forsaken of Such as He Sometime Enjoyed"), and villanelle (Thomas's "Do Not Go Gentle into That Good Night"). Three (by Tennyson, Yeats, and Frost) are in blank verse, and four are irregular as to meter and rhyme, though they do have some meter and rhyme. Only one of the poems—Pound's "The River-

Merchant's Wife: A Letter"—is in genuinely free verse. Meters vary from monometer to hexameter. Despite abundant substitutions and variations, especially in the early feet of a line, only one rhythm is found in these poems: iambic.

The subjects are the subjects that have always engaged our attention: crime and punishment, men and women, love and hate, God and Satan, the seasons, the elements. A goodly number of the poems focus on a brightly charged animal or plant. Among the daffodils, roses, and cherry blossoms we meet a Tyger, a Nightingale, a Windhover, a Swan-god, an Eagle, a Thrush, a Fly, a Snake, and a domestic scene with Cat and Goldfishes.

It touches me that the word "darkling" should occur three times in these hundred poems (used by Keats, Arnold, and Hardy, all writing in the nineteenth century) and practically nowhere else *in the language.* A somber coloration may attend many of these poems, which include a litany, an elegy, an anthem for the doomed, and several valedictions and obituaries. Such beauty as we do manage to achieve is apparently won in the face of a realism that attends our knowledge of our own immediate feebleness and eventual mortality. Any loveliness Frost ever found was accompanied by "dark and deep" hues. Such is the world our favorite poems represent.

I don't know why these hundred poems should be the ones to make it into the exclusive club. I have learned to live with not knowing. I am reminded of a story about a demanding stranger who arrived one morning in a small town and asked a boy on the sidewalk of the main street, "Boy, where's the post office?"

"I don't know."

"Well, then, where might the drugstore be?"

"I don't know."

"How about a good cheap hotel?"

"I don't know."

"Say, boy, you don't know much, do you?"

"No, sir, I sure don't. But I ain't lost."

That's about how I feel when I read through the hundred wonderful poems in this anthology and ask, Why these? I wish I knew, but I don't. But, then, I ain't lost either. One reason I'm not entirely lost is that literature has bestowed on my culture and me a very useful guidebook to what it's like to be alive on earth as a human being. We choose certain poems to go back to time after time, and it seems just as true that the greatest poems are so vital and vivacious that they choose *us* in return and challenge us to earn their great rewards.

1

THE TYGER

~

William Blake

*N*o greater or more suitable poem could stand at the threshold of this col-
lection. "The Tyger" comes from Blake's celebrated *Songs of Experience* (1794).
"The Tyger" is, indeed, vividly and memorably a song of experience. It has
such a powerful rhythm that it seems almost pounded out on a drum or some
other instrument of percussion: something that beats like a heart, or like a
hammer, both of which are named in the poem.

And experience! Blake's tiger is the living embodiment of the fearsome
world of experience that burns, endangering and consuming but also illumi-
nating everything around it. The mighty beast is the whole world of experience
outside ourselves, a world of igneous creation and destruction. Faced with such
terrifying beauty, the poet can only ask questions; the poem is nothing but one
wondering question after another.

The Tyger

Tyger Tyger, burning bright,
In the forests of the night;
What immortal hand or eye,
Could frame thy fearful symmetry?

In what distant deeps or skies
Burnt the fire of thine eyes!
On what wings dare he aspire?
What the hand, dare seize the fire?

And what shoulder, & what art,
Could twist the sinews of thy heart?
And when thy heart began to beat,
What dread hand? & what dread feet?

What the hammer? what the chain,
In what furnace was thy brain?
What the anvil? what dread grasp,
Dare its deadly terrors clasp?

When the stars threw down their spears
And water'd heaven with their tears:
Did he smile his work to see?
Did he who made the Lamb make thee?

Tyger, Tyger burning bright,
In the forests of the night:
What immortal hand or eye,
Dare frame thy fearful symmetry?

2

SIR PATRICK SPENS

~

Anonymous

Samuel Taylor Coleridge's "Dejection: An Ode" has, as epigraph, the "new moon" stanza of this poem; Coleridge begins,

> Well! If the bard was weather-wise, who made
> The grand old ballad of Sir Patrick Spence. . . .

British bards do seem to be weather-wise, living on a northern island where farming and navigation are important. The phases of the moon have to do more with tides than with storms per se, but a rough storm—the sort that comes around the equinoxes or at any time during the winter—will be rougher at the full moon or new moon, when high tides are naturally higher, low tides lower.

This poem and "Edward, Edward" (p. 149) are the only anonymous ballads to qualify for inclusion in this book, and they have some elements in common: both are Scottish, and both strike the note of "blood" early on (figurative here, literal in "Edward, Edward"). But "Sir Patrick Spens" is an altogether more primitive poem: a dramatically elliptical narration in the simplest ballad measure (alternating lines of four and three stresses, rhymed *abcb*) with superlative economy of design—just a few quick bold strokes and a thoroughgoing reliance on concrete detail instead of abstraction. We are not told that the king was worried in some vague way; he is drinking and asking for help. Four brief speeches (king, knight, Sir Patrick, a nameless sailor), and then a focus on the marvelous details of "cork heel'd shoon" (the last word in medieval chic, no doubt) and floating hats.

Sir Patrick Spens

I. THE SAILING

The king sits in Dunfermline town
  Drinking the blude-red wine;
"O whare will I get a skeely skipper
  To sail this new ship o' mine?"

O up and spak an eldern knight,
  Sat at the king's right knee;
"Sir Patrick Spens is the best sailor
  That ever sail'd the sea."

Our king has written a braid letter,
  And seal'd it with his hand,
And sent it to Sir Patrick Spens,
  Was walking on the strand.

"To Noroway, to Noroway,
  To Noroway o'er the faem;
The king's daughter o' Noroway,
  'Tis thou must bring her hame."

The first word that Sir Patrick read
  So loud, loud laugh'd he;
The neist word that Sir Patrick read
  The tear blinded his e'e.

"O wha is this has done this deed
  And tauld the king o' me,
To send us out, at this time o' year,
  To sail upon the sea?

"Be it wind, be it weet, be it hail, be it sleet,
  Our ship must sail the faem;
The king's daughter o' Noroway,
  'Tis we must fetch her hame."

They hoysed their sails on Monenday morn
  Wi' a' the speed they may;
They hae landed in Noroway
  Upon a Wodensday.

II. THE RETURN

"Mak ready, mak ready, my merry men a'!
  Our gude ship sails the morn."
"Now ever alack, my master dear,
  I fear a deadly storm.

"I saw the new moon late yestreen
    Wi' the auld moon in her arm;
And if we gang to sea, master,
    I fear we'll come to harm."

They hadna sail'd a league, a league,
    A league but barely three,
When the lift grew dark, and the wind blew loud,
    And gurly grew the sea.

The ankers brak, and the topmast lap,
    It was sic a deadly storm:
And the waves cam owre the broken ship
    Till a' her sides were torn.

"Go fetch a web o' the silken claith,
    Another o' the twine,
And wap them into our ship's side,
    And let nae the sea come in."

They fetch'd a web o' the silken claith,
    Another o' the twine,
And they wapp'd them round that guide ship's side,
    But still the sea came in.

O laith, laith were our gude Scots lords
    To wet their cork-heel'd shoon;
But lang or a' the play was play'd
    They wat their hats aboon.

And mony was the feather bed
    That flatter'd on the faem;
And mony was the gude lord's son
    That never mair cam hame.

O lang, lang may the ladies sit,
    Wi' their fans into their hand,
Before they see Sir Patrick Spens
    Come sailing to the strand!

And lang, lang may the maidens sit
  Wi' their gowd kames in their hair,
A-waiting for their ain dear loves!
  For them they'll see nae mair.

Half-owre, half-owre to Aberdour,
  'Tis fifty fathoms deep;
And there lies gude Sir Patrick Spens,
  Wi' the Scots lords at his feet!

3

TO AUTUMN

~

John Keats

"*T*o Autumn" is the last of Keats's six great odes. The others, mostly, were written in May of 1819; true to its subject, however, "To Autumn" was written just a day or two before the autumnal equinox of 1819, on September 19.

Keats, perhaps feeling that spring and summer had received too much poetic attention, undertook to write to autumn as a corrective. By the touch of personification, Keats makes autumn "the human season," as it were, not much like the superhuman creativity of spring or the otherworldly extremism of summer and winter.

Keats here exploits to the full his genius for sensual realization—not just how things look and sound but also how they smell, taste, and feel.

To Autumn

I

Season of mists and mellow fruitfulness,
   Close bosom-friend of the maturing sun;
Conspiring with him how to load and bless
   With fruit the vines that round the thatch-eves run;
To bend with apples the mossed cottage-trees,
   And fill all fruit with ripeness to the core;
     To swell the gourd, and plump the hazel shells
With a sweet kernel; to set budding more,
   And still more, later flowers for the bees,
   Until they think warm days will never cease,
     For Summer has o'er-brimmed their clammy cells.

II

Who hath not seen thee oft amid thy store?
   Sometimes whoever seeks abroad may find
Thee sitting careless on a granary floor,
   Thy hair soft-lifted by the winnowing wind;

Or on a half-reaped furrow sound asleep,
   Drowsed with the fume of poppies, while thy hook
     Spares the next swath and all its twinèd flowers:
And sometimes like a gleaner thou dost keep
   Steady thy laden head across a brook;
   Or by a cider-press, with patient look,
     Thou watchest the last oozings hours by hours.

III

Where are the songs of Spring? Ay, where are they?
   Think not of them, thou hast thy music too,—
While barrèd clouds bloom the soft-dying day,
   And touch the stubble-plains with rosy hue;
Then in a wailful choir the small gnats mourn
   Among the river sallows, borne aloft
     Or sinking as the light wind lives or dies;
And full-grown lambs loud bleat from hilly bourn;
   Hedge-crickets sing; and now with treble soft
   The red-breast whistles from a garden-croft;
     And gathering swallows twitter in the skies.

4

THAT TIME OF YEAR THOU MAYST IN ME BEHOLD

~

William Shakespeare

*H*ere is a veritable microcosm of that species of microcosm-parable writing that was very popular in Medieval and Renaissance literature: one life is likened, in order, to a year, a day, and a fire; a man's age is autumnal, crepuscular, moribund. It hardly matters that Shakespeare was less than thirty when he wrote these lines, since, given Elizabethan life expectancy, being twenty-eight or so may be ample justification for a September song.

It is as though the measured pace of poetry implicitly and automatically says, "The clock is ticking, the meter is running"; as Martin Heidegger speculated, we know what time it is because we know we are going to die. At any rate, music and poetry are themselves reminders of time, time is passing, and time's passing adds up finally to a state of inexorable mortality, ever clearer as one ages.

But, as Wallace Stevens was to say in "Sunday Morning" dozens of decades later, "Death is the mother of beauty," and the meter-matrix of mortality gives birth to much of our grandest poetry.

That Time of Year Thou Mayst in Me Behold

That time of year thou mayst in me behold
When yellow leaves, or none, or few, do hang
Upon those boughs which shake against the cold,
Bare ruin'd choirs where late the sweet birds sang.
In me thou see'st the twilight of such day
As after sunset fadeth in the west,
Which by and by black night doth take away,
Death's second self, that seals up all in rest.
In me thou see'st the glowing of such fire
That on the ashes of his youth doth lie,
As the death-bed whereon it must expire,
Consum'd with that which it was nourish'd by.
   This thou perceiv'st, which makes thy love more strong,
   To love that well which thou must leave ere long.

5

PIED BEAUTY

~

Gerard Manley Hopkins

*U*nlike most of the poems in this book, which were published in some form during their authors' lifetimes, those by Hopkins and Emily Dickinson had to wait until some years after their authors' deaths. Strikingly, Hopkins's dates are fairly close to Dickinson's (1830-86); they died only three years apart. Both, moreover, adopted some form of reclusion, she being called, figuratively, the "New England nun," he being literally a Catholic (Jesuit) priest. In the first words of "Pied Beauty"—"Glory be to God"—one hears an echo of the motto of the Jesuit order, *Ad maiorem Dei gloriam,* "To the greater glory of God."

Like Dickinson, Hopkins was an unusual person and a most original poet. Just as "The Windhover" (p. 64) puts a dangerous predator in the place of the meek Dove of conventional Christian symbolism, "Pied Beauty" puts changeable nature, "freckled" and "fickle," in the place of the unchanging spotlessness of a remote Platonic ideal. And, as in "The Windhover" and "God's Grandeur" (p. 77), Hopkins stresses a favorite rhyme of his between "thing" and "wing," as though to say that even in the common and mundane objects and actions of the spotted world there remains the capacity for lofty flight.

Pied Beauty

Glory be to God for dappled things—
    For skies of couple-colour as a brinded cow;
      For rose-moles all in stipple upon trout that swim;
Fresh-firecoal chestnut-falls; finches' wings;
    Landscape plotted and pieced—fold, fallow, and plough;
      And áll trádes, their gear and tackle and trim.
All things counter, original, spare, strange;
    Whatever is fickle, freckled (who knows how?)
      With swift, slow; sweet, sour; adazzle, dim;
He fathers-forth whose beauty is past change:
          Praise him.

6

STOPPING BY WOODS ON A
SNOWY EVENING

~

Robert Frost

It is not clear when the "darkest evening of the year" (line 8) falls: possibly on December 21, the winter solstice, which is the longest period of darkness; or possibly on January 20, traditionally the coldest night of the year. The former possibility would link "Stopping by Woods on a Snowy Evening" with Thomas Hardy's "The Darkling Thrush" (p. 111), which is set on December 31, 1900; the latter possibility recalls John Keats's "The Eve of St. Agnes."

With all three, in any event, the depth of winter, along with evening and night, is made a symbol of hope (in Hardy), love and warmth (in Keats), and loveliness (in Frost).

Frost claimed to have written this poem almost effortlessly in the morning after staying up all night to work on his long poem "New Hampshire" (a pattern rather like Rainer Maria Rilke's devotion of much time to his *Duino Elegies* after which he wrote the very different *Sonnets to Orpheus* almost without needing to think).

The thirteenth line has provoked some puzzlement. The arrangement of adjectives could suggest that the woods are lovely and dark and deep, or that they are lovely because they are dark and deep. Algebraically, we could have

$$(x + y + z)$$

or

$$x + (y + z)$$

I hold with those who favor the second reading, which adds a measure of subtlety lacking from the simpler sequence.

Stopping by Woods on a Snowy Evening

Whose woods these are I think I know.
His house is in the village, though;
He will not see me stopping here
To watch his woods fill up with snow.

My little horse must think it queer
To stop without a farmhouse near
Between the woods and frozen lake
The darkest evening of the year.

He gives his harness bells a shake
To ask if there is some mistake.
The only other sound's the sweep
Of easy wind and downy flake.

The woods are lovely, dark and deep,
But I have promises to keep,
And miles to go before I sleep,
And miles to go before I sleep.

7

KUBLA KHAN

~

Samuel Taylor Coleridge

Coleridge's candid-seeming account of the genesis of "Kubla Khan" is almost as famous as the poem itself (see p. 214), and the anonymous "person on business from Porlock" has achieved a notoriety of his or her own, even among modern poets (see Stevie Smith's "Thoughts about the Person from Porlock" and Amy Clampitt's "A Cure at Porlock").

The origins of "Kubla Khan" and "The Rime of the Ancient Mariner" (p. 161) are the subject of one of the most famous critical studies of the twentieth century, John Livingston Lowes's *The Road to Xanadu,* originally published in 1927.

Fundamentally, we have in Coleridge a genius-level mentality at about the age of twenty-five (in 1797), with his deep desires given special form and color by fabulously comprehensive reading and profound thinking. The desires take the form of a Paradise, which literally means "a walled enclosure." (The late Commissioner of Baseball, A. Bartlett Giamatti, who had been a professor of literature, noted that descriptions of "paradise" sound a good deal like a ballpark.) Then, reading in a book about another walled enclosure devoted to pleasure, the genius falls asleep, lulled by both opium and the charms of repeated esoteric sounds:

> In Xanadu did Kubla Khan

The result is the most magnificent representation in English of what dreams and visions are like—no matter how fragmentary.

Kubla Khan

Or, a Vision in a Dream. A Fragment.

In Xanadu did Kubla Khan
A stately pleasure-dome decree:
Where Alph, the sacred river, ran
Through caverns measureless to man
    Down to a sunless sea.
So twice five miles of fertile ground

With walls and towers were girdled round;
And there were gardens bright with sinuous rills,
Where blossomed many an incense-bearing tree;
And here were forests ancient as the hills,
Enfolding sunny spots of greenery.

But oh! that deep romantic chasm which slanted
Down the green hill athwart a cedarn cover!
A savage place! as holy and enchanted
As e'er beneath a waning moon was haunted
By woman wailing for her demon-lover!
And from this chasm, with ceaseless turmoil seething,
As if this earth in fast thick pants were breathing,
A mighty fountain momently was forced:
Amid whose swift half-intermitted burst
Huge fragments vaulted like rebounding hail,
Or chaffy grain beneath the thresher's flail:
And 'mid these dancing rocks at once and ever
It flung up momently the sacred river.
Five miles meandering with a mazy motion
Through wood and dale the sacred river ran,
Then reached the caverns measureless to man,
And sank in tumult to a lifeless ocean:
And 'mid this tumult Kubla heard from far
Ancestral voices prophesying war!

The shadow of the dome of pleasure
Floated midway on the waves;
Where was heard the mingled measure
From the fountain and the caves.
It was a miracle of rare device,
A sunny pleasure-dome with caves of ice!

A damsel with a dulcimer
In a vision once I saw:
It was an Abyssinian maid,
And on her dulcimer she played,
Singing of Mount Abora.
Could I revive within me
Her symphony and song,
To such a deep delight 'twould win me,

That with music loud and long,
I would build that dome in air,
That sunny dome! those caves of ice!
And all who heard should see them there,
And all should cry, Beware! Beware!
His flashing eyes, his floating hair!
Weave a circle round him thrice,
And close your eyes with holy dread,
For he on honey-dew hath fed,
And drunk the milk of Paradise.

8

DOVER BEACH

~

Matthew Arnold

---

*A*lthough it was written in the middle of the nineteenth century, "Dover Beach" has some claim to be the first distinctly modern poem and may even qualify as "modernist" in the way it places an isolated neurotic on the edge of a highly charged symbolic landscape and seascape with beach, full moon, and high tide. The lines are broken and uneven, and some of the transitions are abrupt, almost surrealist. And there may be an ironic self-contradiction in the tender exhortation, "Ah, love, let us be true/ To one another!" If the world has no love or certitude, then there is no way for even love to be true.

Among poems about people and the sea, T. S. Eliot's "The Love Song of J. Alfred Prufrock" (p. 55) and "The Dry Salvages," Wallace Stevens's "The Idea of Order at Key West," and A. R. Ammons's "Corsons Inlet" are outstanding.

The Aegean Sea, being tideless, could not have reminded Sophocles of the ebb and flow of human misery. But that pedantic cheap shot ignores the fact that the Aegean Sea in this poem does indeed, by artistic fiat, have tides. This is not an oceanographic article, but a somber love poem.

Dover Beach

The sea is calm tonight.
The tide is full, the moon lies fair
Upon the straits;—on the French coast the light
Gleams and is gone; the cliffs of England stand,
Glimmering and vast, out in the tranquil bay.
Come to the window, sweet is the night-air!
Only, from the long line of spray
Where the sea meets the moon-blanched land,
Listen! you hear the grating roar
Of pebbles which the waves draw back, and fling,
At their return, up the high strand,
Begin, and cease, and then again begin,
With tremulous cadence slow, and bring
The eternal note of sadness in.

Sophocles long ago
Heard it on the Aegean, and it brought
Into his mind the turbid ebb and flow
Of human misery; we
Find also in the sound a thought,
Hearing it by this distant northern sea.

The Sea of Faith
Was once, too, at the full, and round earth's shore
Lay like the folds of a bright girdle furled.
But now I only hear
Its melancholy, long, withdrawing roar,
Retreating, to the breath
Of the night-wind, down the vast edges drear
And naked shingles of the world.

Ah, love, let us be true
To one another! for the world, which seems
To lie before us like a land of dreams,
So various, so beautiful, so new,
Hath really neither joy, nor love, nor light,
Nor certitude, nor peace, nor help for pain;
And we are here as on a darkling plain
Swept with confused alarms of struggle and flight,
Where ignorant armies clash by night.

9

LA BELLE DAME SANS MERCI

~

John Keats

---

*I*n "The Eve of St. Agnes," a poem Keats wrote before he wrote "La Belle Dame sans Merci," the meeting of Porphyro and Madeline includes music:

> Awakening up, he took her hollow lute—
> Tumultuous—and, in chords that tenderest be,
> He played an ancient ditty, long since mute,
> In Provence called *"La belle dame sans merci"* . . . .

Scholars have taken this to mean a medieval song by Alain Chartier the title of which can be translated as "The Lovely Lady Without Pity."

The *femme fatale* is a favorite character, as we can see from the stories of Judith, Delilah, Cleopatra, Salome, and their modern counterparts in *Of Human Bondage* and *The Blue Angel.*

A slightly earlier generation of poets than Keats's—including Robert Burns, William Blake, William Wordsworth, Sir Walter Scott, Samuel Taylor Coleridge, and Lord Byron—had participated in the revival of ballad-writing. Burns and Scott did a good deal of adapting and revising—as "Auld Lang Syne," say, is partly Burns's work and partly that of anonymous folk-composers.

For "La Belle Dame sans Merci," Keats borrowed a medieval title (though nothing of Chartier's substance) and adapted the standard ballad stanza; he also followed the ballad convention—which can be seen in "Edward, Edward" (p. 149)—of casting the entire poem in the form of a dialogue with questions and answers.

Keats wrote two versions of this strangely powerful story. Since they are short, and since critics differ about which is better, both are given here.

La Belle Dame sans Merci

> O what can ail thee, Knight at arms,
>   Alone and palely loitering?
> The sedge has withered from the Lake
>   And no birds sing!

O what can ail thee, Knight at arms,
  So haggard, and so woe begone?
The Squirrel's granary is full
  And the harvest's done.

I see a lily on thy brow
  With anguish moist and fever dew,
And on thy cheeks a fading rose
  Fast withereth too—

I met a Lady in the Meads,
  Full beautiful, a faery's child
Her hair was long, her foot was light
  And her eyes were wild—

I made a Garland for her head,
  And bracelets too, and fragrant Zone
She look'd at me as she did love
  And made sweet moan—

I set her on my pacing steed
  And nothing else saw all day long
For sidelong would she bend and sing
  A faery's song—

She found me roots of relish sweet
  And honey wild and manna dew
And sure in language strange she said
  I love thee true—

She took me to her elfin grot
  And there she wept and sigh'd full sore,
And there I shut her wild wild eyes
  With kisses four.

And there she lulled me asleep
  And there I dream'd, Ah Woe betide!
The latest dream I ever dreamt
  On the cold hill side.

I saw pale Kings, and Princes too
    Pale warriors, death pale were they all;
They cried, La belle dame sans merci
    Hath thee in thrall.

I saw their starv'd lips in the gloam
    With horrid warning gaped wide,
And I awoke, and found me here
    On the cold hill's side.

And this is why I sojourn here
    Alone and palely loitering;
Though the sedge is withered from the Lake
    And no birds sing—

La Belle Dame sans Merci (Revised Version)

Ah, what can ail thee, wretched wight,
    Alone and palely loitering;
The sedge has wither'd from the lake,
    And no birds sing.

Ah, what can ail thee, wretched wight,
    So haggard and so woe-begone?
The squirrel's granary is full,
    And the harvest's done.

I see a lilly on thy brow,
    With anguish moist and fever dew;
And on thy cheek a fading rose
    Fast withereth too.

I met a Lady in the meads
    Full beautiful, a fairy's child;
Her hair was long, her foot was light,
    And her eyes were wild.

I set her on my pacing steed,
    And nothing else saw all day long;
For sideways would she lean, and sing
    A faery's song.

I made a garland for her head,
   And bracelets too, and fragrant zone;
She look'd at me as she did love,
   And made sweet moan.

She found me roots of relish sweet,
   And honey wild, and manna dew,
And sure in language strange she said,
   I love thee true.

She took me to her elfin grot,
   And there she gaz'd and sighed deep,
And there I shut her wild sad eyes—
   So kiss'd to sleep.

And there we slumber'd on the moss,
   And there I dream'd, ah woe betide
The latest dream I ever dream'd
   On the cold hill side.

I saw pale kings, and princes too,
   Pale warriors, death-pale were they all;
Who cry'd—"La belle Dame sans mercy
   Hath thee in thrall!"

I saw their starv'd lips in the gloom
   With horrid warning gaped wide,
And I awoke, and found me here
   On the cold hill side.

And this is why I sojourn here
   Alone and palely loitering,
Though the sedge is wither'd from the lake,
   And no birds sing.

10

TO THE VIRGINS, TO MAKE MUCH
OF TIME

~

Robert Herrick

As the teacher portrayed by Robin Williams in the film *Dead Poets Society* pointed out to his students, "To the Virgins, to Make Much of Time" partakes of the antique convention known as *carpe diem,* "seize the day." And Herrick's gem of a poem is a good deal like Andrew Marvell's *carpe diem* poem "To His Coy Mistress" (p. 27).

But unlike Marvell's clever pseudo-syllogism, Herrick's little song simply asserts a set of pretty hackneyed propositions, including a variant of "time flies," followed by the imperatives "be not coy," "use your time," and "go marry." It sounds as though Herrick would not necessarily insist on the marrying, either.

To the Virgins, to Make Much of Time

Gather ye rose-buds while ye may,
    Old Time is still a-flying;
And this same flower that smiles today,
    Tomorrow will be dying.

The glorious lamp of heaven, the sun,
    The higher he's a-getting,
The sooner will his race be run,
    And nearer he's to setting.

That age is best which is the first,
    When youth and blood are warmer;
But being spent, the worse, and worst
    Times still succeed the former.

Then be not coy, but use your time,
    And while ye may, go marry;
For having lost but once your prime,
    You may for ever tarry.

11

TO HIS COY MISTRESS

~

Andrew Marvell

T. S. Eliot noticed that this great poem of seduction has a lucidly logical structure:

1. If we had time, you could hold out.
2. We don't have time.
3. "Now therefore . . ."

Such a combination of mechanical logic and passionate feeling is typical of the witty "Metaphysical" poetry fashionable throughout the seventeenth century and again in the twentieth.

Like Herrick's "To the Virgins, to Make Much of Time," this poem belongs to the category of *carpe diem:* seize the day. In truth it may be a fantastically exaggerated mockery of the *carpe diem* conventions for the purpose of praise, as though to say, "You are so beautiful that I could conceive an exponentially silly argument, thus. . . ."

To His Coy Mistress

Had we but world enough and time,
This coyness, lady, were no crime.
We would sit down and think which way
To walk, and pass our long love's day.
Thou by the Indian Ganges' side
Should'st rubies find; I by the tide
Of Humber would complain. I would
Love you ten years before the Flood,
And you should, if you please, refuse
Till the conversion of the Jews.
My vegetable love should grow
Vaster than empires, and more slow.
An hundred years should go to praise
Thine eyes, and on thy forehead gaze,
Two hundred to adore each breast,

But thirty thousand to the rest.
An age at least to every part,
And the last age should show your heart.
For, lady, you deserve this state,
Nor would I love at lower rate.

But at my back I always hear
Time's winged chariot hurrying near,
And yonder all before us lie
Deserts of vast eternity.
Thy beauty shall no more be found,
Nor in thy marble vault shall sound
My echoing song; then worms shall try
That long preserved virginity,
And your quaint honor turn to dust,
And into ashes all my lust.
The grave's a fine and private place,
But none, I think, do there embrace.

Now therefore, while the youthful hue
Sits on thy skin like morning glew
And while thy willing soul transpires
At every pore with instant fires,
Now let us sport us while we may;
And now, like amorous birds of prey,
Rather at once our time devour
Than languish in his slow-chapped power.
Let us roll all our strength and all
Our sweetness up into one ball
And tear our pleasures with rough strife
Thorough the iron gates of life.
Thus, though we cannot make our sun
Stand still, yet we will make him run.

12

THE PASSIONATE SHEPHERD TO
HIS LOVE
~
Christopher Marlowe

*I*t seems unlikely that any poem in English has set off such a widespread and long-lasting reaction; and that is probably what Marlowe had in mind, for he was an extraordinarily dramatic, dynamic, and polemical genius.

Marlowe's gentle pseudo-pastoral was first published after his death, in a collection called *The Passionate Pilgrim* in 1599. The next year, in *England's Helicon,* the poem appeared along with a reply, "The Nymph's Reply to the Shepherd," possibly by Sir Walter Ralegh, including the disdainful lines:

> Thy gowns, thy shoes, thy beds of roses,
> Thy cap, thy kirtle, and thy posies,
> Soon break, soon wither—soon forgotten,
> In folly ripe, in reason rotten.

In 1633 John Donne offered his response in "The Bait":

> Come live with me and be my love,
> And we will some new pleasures prove,
> Of golden sands and crystal brooks,
> With silken lines and silver hooks.

Three centuries later, the debate is still in progress. In a poem called "Raleigh Was Right," William Carlos Williams added his skeptical voice: "We cannot go to the country/ for the country will bring us no peace."

C. Day Lewis produced a more or less Marxist variation (in "Two Songs"):

> Come, live with me and be my love,
> And we will all the pleasures prove
> Of peace and plenty, bed and board,
> That chance employment may afford.

Delmore Schwartz and Paul Engle each wrote a poem beginning "Come live with me and be my wife."

And in Peter DeVries's novel *The Tents of Wickedness* (1959), a character called Beth Appleyard composes "Bacchanal," which begins

"Come live with me and be my love,"
He said, in substance. "There's no vine
We will not pluck the clusters of,
Or grape we will not turn to wine."

Marlowe, a wonderfully witty man, must be getting a kick out of the whole thing, whether in hell or heaven.

The Passionate Shepherd to His Love

Come live with me and be my love,
And we will all the pleasures prove
That valleys, groves, hills, and fields,
Woods, or steepy mountain yields.

And we will sit upon the rocks,
Seeing the shepherds feed their flocks
By shallow rivers, to whose falls
Melodious birds sing madrigals.

And I will make thee beds of roses
And a thousand fragrant posies,
A cap of flowers and a kirtle
Embroidered all with leaves of myrtle;

A gown made of the finest wool
Which from our pretty lambs we pull;
Fair-lined slippers for the cold,
With buckles of the purest gold;

A belt of straw and ivy buds,
With coral clasps and amber studs.
And if these pleasures may thee move,
Come live with me and be my love.

The shepherds' swains shall dance and sing
For thy delight each May morning.
If these delights thy mind may move,
Then live with me and be my love.

13

DEATH, BE NOT PROUD

~

John Donne

---

*T*hree of Donne's "Holy Sonnets" are included here: this (the tenth), the seventh, and the fourteenth (pp. 69 and 155). They are much alike, especially in their common reliance on imperatives, dramatic paradoxes, and subtle-seeming ratiocination. The notion of the death of death resembles such other "of" redundancies as the definition of "definition." It teases the mind terribly: if death can die, then death is not dead.

Even so, we can imagine the famous preacher, in an age of great preaching and also of great theater and political drama, personifying and addressing Death, starting with a stern admonition, passing on to feigned sympathy for "poor" deluded Death, dropping to a hushed tone with talk of rest and sleep, winding up with a riveting peroration: "Thou art slave to fate, chance, kings, and desperate men."

Death, Be Not Proud

Death, be not proud, though some have called thee
Mighty and dreadful, for thou art not so;
For those whom thou think'st thou dost overthrow
Die not, poor Death, nor yet canst thou kill me.
From rest and sleep, which but thy pictures be,
Much pleasure; then from thee much more must flow,
And soonest our best men with thee do go,
Rest of their bones, and soul's delivery.
Thou art slave to fate, chance, kings, and desperate men,
And dost with poison, war, and sickness dwell;
And poppy or charms can make us sleep as well
And better than thy stroke; why swell'st thou then?
One short sleep past, we wake eternally,
And death shall be no more; Death, thou shalt die.

14

UPON JULIA'S CLOTHES

~

Robert Herrick

*A*mong the 1200 poems that Herrick wrote, we find "Julia's Petticoat," "The Night-Piece, to Julia," two or three called simply "To Julia," "Upon His Julia," "Upon Julia Washing Herself in the River," "Upon Julia's Breasts," "Upon Julia's Fall," "Upon Julia's Ribband," "Upon Julia's Voice," and this one—all overwhelming evidence that Julia complained about being neglected.

The highlights of the poem are the surprisingly technical term "liquefaction" and the brilliant stroke (abetted by alliteration) of "brave vibration" (this is "brave" as in "brave new world": i.e., *splendid*).

Upon Julia's Clothes

Whenas in silks my Julia goes,
Then, then, methinks, how sweetly flows
That liquefaction of her clothes.

Next, when I cast mine eyes and see
That brave vibration, each way free,
O how that glittering taketh me!

15

TO LUCASTA, GOING TO THE WARS
~
Richard Lovelace

"*L*ucasta" was, presumably, Lovelace's poetic name for his fiancée, whose real name was Lucy Sacheverell. He did, in fact, love honor more than Lucasta; and he did, in fact, go to war. And when, by an error, his death was reported to her, she married somebody else.

Here we can see, in a small way, some of the outlandish figures or "conceits" that seventeenth-century poets were so crazy about: the chaste breast and quiet mind of the beloved likened to a nunnery, the "first foe in the field" converted into a most unlikely "mistress," and military paraphernalia made the articles of a stronger faith.

The argument may seem quaint and even silly today, when ideals of chivalry and honor have just about perished, or at least have lost any relevance in time of war. A Lysistrata—ancient (as in Aristophanes' comedy) or contemporary— might retort that the speaker of the poem may love warfare more (else he wouldn't have thought of the foe as a "new mistress") and that he may love the idea of going, but that honor has nothing to do with it.

To Lucasta, Going to the Wars

Tell me not, Sweet, I am unkind
   That from the nunnery
Of thy chaste breast and quiet mind,
   To war and arms I fly.

True, a new mistress now I chase,
   The first foe in the field;
And with a stronger faith embrace
   A sword, a horse, a shield.

Yet this inconstancy is such
   As you too shall adore;
I could not love thee, Dear, so much,
   Loved I not Honor more.

16

THE WORLD IS TOO MUCH
WITH US
~
William Wordsworth

*I*t was Wordsworth's good fortune to be entrusted with the resuscitation of the sonnet, a form that had gone somewhat into eclipse and disfavor after the death of Milton. The form refers back to sixteenth- and seventeenth-century precursors, and some of the imagery refers back as well: the description of Proteus (the Old Man of the Sea) recalls Milton's description of Proteus; that of the sea-god Triton recalls Spenser's.

Wordsworth was a pious Christian, so it is hard to say how serious or how ironic he is here when he indicates a preference for Paganism if its animistic polytheism could give him a better sense of Nature, as opposed to "the world" of human affairs.

The World Is Too Much with Us

The world is too much with us; late and soon,
Getting and spending, we lay waste our powers:
Little we see in Nature that is ours;
We have given our hearts away, a sordid boon!
This Sea that bares her bosom to the moon;
The winds that will be howling at all hours,
And are up-gathered now like sleeping flowers;
For this, for everything, we are out of tune;
It moves us not. — Great God! I'd rather be
A Pagan suckled in a creed outworn;
So might I, standing on this pleasant lea,
Have glimpses that would make me less forlorn;
Have sight of Proteus rising from the sea;
Or hear old Triton blow his wreathed horn.

17

ON FIRST LOOKING INTO CHAPMAN'S HOMER

~

John Keats

A personal aside: as I am writing this note, on August 23, 1989, the Voyager 2 spacecraft is sending back extraordinarily clear and detailed pictures of Neptune, and even jaded astronomers are jumping with joy at all the newly discovered satellites, rings, storms, and other features of the planet.

Keats made two very apt choices of metaphors for his excitement at getting a glimpse of Homer, whose Greek he could not read, through the translations of Chapman, whose English very few read today. Keats erred in giving Cortez credit for what Balboa in fact did, but it was brilliant of him to connect the Renaissance explorers with the more recent scientific discoverers.

It may be that Homer's so-called epic similes—extended metaphors with many details—inspired Keats to find two new similes for his own feeling on first *looking into* (the idiom is both casual and profound) Chapman's Homer.

On First Looking into Chapman's Homer

Much have I traveled in the realms of gold,
    And many goodly states and kingdoms seen;
    Round many western islands have I been
Which bards in fealty to Apollo hold.
Oft of one wide expanse had I been told
    That deep-browed Homer ruled as his demesne,
    Yet did I never breathe its pure serene
Till I heard Chapman speak out loud and bold.
Then felt I like some watcher of the skies
    When a new planet swims into his ken;
Or like stout Cortez when with eagle eyes
    He stared at the Pacific—and all his men
Looked at each other with a wild surmise—
    Silent, upon a peak in Darien.

18

JABBERWOCKY

~

"Lewis Carroll"
(Charles Lutwidge Dodgson)

*T*his poem—a version of which Lewis Carroll wrote earlier as a joke "Stanza of Anglo-Saxon Poetry"—comes in *Through the Looking-Glass,* where it is read by Alice and explicated by Humpty Dumpty. It is called "nonsense," but that seems to be a misnomer. In absolute nonsense, nothing would have any meaning—the words would not really be words. In relative nonsense, some of the words may have some meaning: this is the experience of all children and many foreigners when they first hear a language. One struggles to impose sense, but much of what one hears sounds like "The ummghph of the nrrghsion seems to be largely a hynnctiousness of frubjubirtude," etc.

Lewis Carroll, much like Jonathan Swift and Edgar Allan Poe, seems to have had direct access to the secrets of childhood, with all its repressed anxieties about size and identity (among the main concerns of *Gulliver's Travels* as well as the *Alice* books), and he could write some very sensible nonsense, wherein we may not know exactly what some words mean but will know (guided by the verse) how they sound and (guided by the syntax) what parts of speech are represented (e.g., "mome raths outgrabe" is the standard adjective-noun-verb sequence). Formation of words by the "portmanteau" device has become common, as in "motel," "smog," and "palimony." If you will look up the derivation of "culprit," you will see that English has been making portmanteau words for centuries. "Chortle," coined here by Carroll, is now in the language.

Jabberwocky

'Twas brillig, and the slithy toves
  Did gyre and gimble in the wabe;
All mimsy were the borogoves,
  And the mome raths outgrabe.

"Beware the Jabberwock, my son!
    The jaws that bite, the claws that catch!
Beware the Jubjub bird, and shun
    The frumious Bandersnatch!"

He took his vorpal sword in hand:
    Long time the manxome foe he sought —
So rested he by the Tumtum tree,
    And stood awhile in thought.

And as in uffish thought he stood,
    The Jabberwock, with eyes of flame,
Came whiffling through the tulgey wood,
    And burbled as it came!

One, two! One, two! And through and through
    The vorpal blade went snicker-snack!
He left it dead, and with its head
    He went galumphing back.

"And hast thou slain the Jabberwock!
    Come to my arms, my beamish boy!
O frabjous day! Callooh! Callay!"
    He chortled in his joy.

'Twas brillig, and the slithy toves
    Did gyre and gimble in the wabe;
All mimsy were the borogoves,
    And the mome raths outgrabe.

19

THE SECOND COMING

~

William Butler Yeats

*N*orman Mailer recognized "The Second Coming" as the greatest lyric poem of the twentieth century, and he was most likely responding to two antithetical qualities that Yeats and his poetry combined.

On the one hand, Yeats seemed to entertain the most fantastic beliefs in the supernatural, all the way from harmless parlor games to a most solemn theory of recurrences in human history. No species of mumbo jumbo, however squalid its proponents or outlandish its principles, escaped Yeats's sympathetic attention. On the other hand, he could confront the most pressing of actual problems in the real world of commerce and politics (and was later a member of the Senate of the Republic of Ireland).

"The Second Coming" feints in the direction of mumbo jumbo in its reference to *Spiritus Mundi,* a "spirit of the world" that contains or generates the images and symbols found in dreams and rituals, all rather fabulous and escapist. (Like Dante and Whitman, Yeats was a Gemini: divided in mind and heart in some ways but not given to skepticism for long.) But against this farfetched world of sphinxes and poppycock, there is a picture of Yeats struggling with the greatest problem of the modern world: war.

The irony is that this second coming is hardly the peace-bringing Second Coming of Christ but rather the reappearance of a terrible beast. The "rocking cradle" seems to be the desert birthplace of many religions, and the rocking comes from world-shaking conflict in a part of the world that, thousands of years ago and this very day as well, fifty years after Yeats's death, has seen little but strife.

The Second Coming

Turning and turning in the widening gyre
The falcon cannot hear the falconer;
Things fall apart; the center cannot hold;
Mere anarchy is loosed upon the world,
The blood-dimmed tide is loosed, and everywhere

The ceremony of innocence is drowned;
The best lack all conviction, while the worst
Are full of passionate intensity.

Surely some revelation is at hand;
Surely the Second Coming is at hand.
The Second Coming! Hardly are those words out
When a vast image out of *Spiritus Mundi*
Troubles my sight: somewhere in sands of the desert
A shape with lion body and the head of a man,
A gaze blank and pitiless as the sun,
Is moving its slow thighs, while all about it
Reel shadows of the indignant desert birds.
The darkness drops again; but now I know
That twenty centuries of stony sleep
Were vexed to nightmare by a rocking cradle,
And what rough beast, its hour come round at last,
Slouches towards Bethlehem to be born?

20

ELEGY WRITTEN IN A COUNTRY CHURCHYARD

~

Thomas Gray

*T*here are probably twenty poets in English greater than Thomas Gray, but only two or three of them have been more influential. Gray's lines reach us through such titles as Thomas Hardy's *Far from the Madding Crowd* and Humphrey Cobb's *Paths of Glory,* as well as through overt echoes and allusions in T. S. Eliot, John Crowe Ransom, Hart Crane, and Philip Larkin.

Gray's execution of the conventions of the heroic quatrain is virtually flawless, and he provides many a bonus to the jaded ear. In the "storied urn" stanza, for instance, the rhyme-words "bust," "breath," "dust," and "death" furnish rhyme in an *abab* pattern but also are joined by alliteration in an *aabb* pattern. The sentence "all the air a solemn stillness holds" also provides *aabb* alliteration and, remarkably, is reversible: "stillness" can be both subject and object of "holds."

Since the composition of the poem took something like nine years, it is not factually true that it—or all of it, at any rate—was written in a country churchyard. The imaginative use of the present tense, the brooding poet-speaker, the democratic-populist sentiments all mark the poem as "proto-Romantic," a precursor of Wordsworth by about fifty years. The meditative poem set in a sacred place continues through Wordsworth's "Tintern Abbey," Hardy's "The Darkling Thrush" (p. 111), Eliot's "Little Gidding," and Larkin's "Church Going."

Elegy Written in a Country Churchyard

The curfew tolls the knell of parting day,
    The lowing herd wind slowly o'er the lea,
The plowman homeward plods his weary way,
    And leaves the world to darkness and to me.

Now fades the glimmering landscape on the sight,
    And all the air a solemn stillness holds,
Save where the beetle wheels his droning flight,
    And drowsy tinklings lull the distant folds;

Save that from yonder ivy-mantled tower
  The moping owl does to the moon complain
Of such as, wand'ring near her secret bower,
  Molest her ancient solitary reign.

Beneath those rugged elms, that yew tree's shade,
  Where heaves the turf in many a mold'ring heap,
Each in his narrow cell forever laid,
  The rude forefathers of the hamlet sleep.

The breezy call of incense-breathing morn,
  The swallow twitt'ring from the straw-built shed,
The cock's shrill clarion, or the echoing horn,
  No more shall rouse them from their lowly bed.

For them no more the blazing hearth shall burn,
  Or busy housewife ply her evening care;
No children run to lisp their sire's return,
  Or climb his knees the envied kiss to share.

Oft did the harvest to their sickle yield,
  Their furrow oft the stubborn glebe has broke;
How jocund did they drive their team afield!
  How bowed the woods beneath their sturdy stroke!

Let not Ambition mock their useful toil,
  Their homely joys, and destiny obscure;
Nor Grandeur hear with a disdainful smile
  The short and simple annals of the poor.

The boast of heraldry, the pomp of pow'r,
  And all that beauty, all that wealth e'er gave,
Awaits alike th' inevitable hour.
  The paths of glory lead but to the grave.

Nor you, ye proud, impute to these the fault,
  If Mem'ry o'er their tomb no trophies raise,
Where through the long-drawn aisle and fretted vault
  The pealing anthem swells the note of praise.

Can storied urn or animated bust
  Back to its mansion call the fleeting breath?
Can Honor's voice provoke the silent dust,
  Or Flatt'ry soothe the dull cold ear of Death?

Perhaps in this neglected spot is laid
  Some heart once pregnant with celestial fire;
Hands that the rod of empire might have swayed,
  Or waked to ecstasy the living lyre.

But knowledge to their eyes her ample page
  Rich with the spoils of time did ne'er unroll;
Chill Penury repressed their noble rage,
  And froze the genial current of the soul.

Full many a gem of purest ray serene,
  The dark unfathomed caves of ocean bear:
Full many a flower is born to blush unseen,
  And waste its sweetness on the desert air.

Some village Hampden, that with dauntless breast
  The little tyrant of his field withstood;
Some mute inglorious Milton here may rest,
  Some Cromwell, guiltless of his country's blood.

Th' applause of list'ning senates to command,
  The threats of pain and ruin to despise,
To scatter plenty o'er a smiling land,
  And read their hist'ry in a nation's eyes,

Their lot forbade; nor circumscribed alone
  Their glowing virtues, but their crimes confined;
Forbade to wade through slaughter to a throne,
  And shut the gates of mercy on mankind,

The struggling pangs of conscious truth to hide,
  To quench the blushes of ingenuous shame,
Or heap the shrine of Luxury and Pride
  With incense kindled at the Muse's flame.

Far from the madding crowd's ignoble strife,
  Their sober wishes never learned to stray;
Along the cool sequestered vale of life
  They kept the noiseless tenor of their way.

Yet ev'n these bones from insult to protect
  Some frail memorial still erected nigh,
With uncouth rhymes and shapeless sculpture decked,
  Implores the passing tribute of a sigh.

Their name, their years, spelt by th' unlettered Muse,
  The place of fame and elegy supply:
And many a holy text around she strews,
  That teach the rustic moralist to die.

For who to dumb Forgetfulness a prey,
  This pleasing anxious being e'er resigned,
Left the warm precincts of the cheerful day,
  Nor cast one longing ling'ring look behind?

On some fond breast the parting soul relies,
  Some pious drops the closing eye requires;
Ev'n from the tomb the voice of Nature cries,
  Ev'n in our ashes live their wonted fires.

For thee, who mindful of th' unhonored dead
  Dost in these lines their artless tale relate;
If chance, by lonely contemplation led,
  Some kindred spirit shall inquire thy fate,

Haply some hoary-headed swain may say,
  "Oft have we seen him at the peep of dawn
Brushing with hasty steps the dews away
  To meet the sun upon the upland lawn.

"There at the foot of yonder nodding beech
  That wreathes its old fantastic roots so high,
His listless length at noontide would he stretch,
  And pore upon the brook that babbles by.

"Hard by yon wood, now smiling as in scorn,
    Mutt'ring has wayward fancies he would rove,
Now dropping, woeful wan, like one forlorn,
    Or crazed with care, or crossed in hopeless love.

"One morn I missed him, on the customed hill,
    Along the heath and near his fav'rite tree;
Another came; not yet beside the rill,
    Nor up the lawn, nor at the wood was he;

"The next with dirges due in sad array
    Slow though the churchway path we saw him borne.
Approach and read (for thou canst read) the lay,
    Graved on the stone beneath yon aged thorn."

The Epitaph

Here rests his head upon the lap of Earth
    A youth to Fortune and to Fame unknown.
Fair Science frowned not on his humble birth,
    And Melancholy marked him for her own.

Large was his bounty, and his soul sincere,
    Heav'n did a recompense as largely send:
He gave to Mis'ry all he had, a tear,
    He gained from Heav'n ('twas all he wished) a friend.

No farther seek his merits to disclose,
    Or draw his frailties from their dread abode,
(There they alike in trembling hope repose),
    The bosom of His Father and his God.

21

OZYMANDIAS

~

Percy Bysshe Shelley

*T*he joke seems to be on Ozymandias, of whose boasting nothing remains but some fragments in a legend; the moral, thus far, seems sound: take care how you brag.

But maybe the joke is on somebody besides the king. For one thing, he— a.k.a. Ramses II of Egypt—may still endure as a mummy. And, even if the great statue is broken and the inscription sounds fatuous, what remains of anybody else of that age? Vain or not, he remains the king to whom a superlative poet devoted a great poem—whereupon, all over again, we may look on his works and despair, so that the joke may be, in part, on ourselves.

Ozymandias

I met a traveler from an antique land
Who said: Two vast and trunkless legs of stone
Stand in the desert. Near them, on the sand,
Half sunk, a shattered visage lies, whose frown,
And wrinkled lip, and sneer of cold command,
Tell that its sculptor well those passions read
Which yet survive, stamped on these lifeless things,
The hand that mocked them and the heart that fed;
And on the pedestal these words appear:
"My name is Ozymandias, king of kings:
Look on my works, ye Mighty, and despair!"
Nothing beside remains. Round the decay
Of that colossal wreck, boundless and bare
The lone and level sands stretch far away.

22

SAILING TO BYZANTIUM

~

William Butler Yeats

*I*n his much earlier poem "The Lake Isle of Innisfree" (p. 182), Yeats had implied that Dublin was no city for young men whose romantic hearts were saturated with longings and yearnings, their minds soaked in the anti-urban polemics of Thoreau's *Walden*. Never mind that Yeats's vision came from a book and not from actual experience; never mind, as well, that he did not arise and go to Innisfree: the point is that he could make a vivid and dramatic poem out of longings that, for almost everybody, must remain inchoate or mute.

In his fertile maturity, from about the age of fifty until his death at seventy-three, Yeats achieved a loftier view, at once more realistic *and* more idealistic. What is rejected is not the usual "world" ("too much with us") of "getting and spending" in the modern urban commercial scientific spirit but rather the biological world of spending and begetting; what is sought is not the rural peace of a small island in a beautiful lake but the concentrated unity of life in an ideal city, medieval Byzantium (which was the name of the place until A.D. 330, when it became Constantinople, changed in 1930 to Istanbul—but a note by Yeats suggests that he has in mind the city as it was in the sixth century). As with most modern medievalism, Yeats's powerful vision attributes unity and synthesis to life in a city that mixed east and west, north and south, Asia and Europe, Christian and pagan (and later Islamic) theology; along with unity of art, philosophy, craft, government, and education. "The Lake of Isle of Innisfree" is spoken as though from the perspective of Dublin before the escape; "Sailing by Byzantium" is spoken as though from the perspective of Byzantium after the escape has been effected.

Sailing to Byzantium

I

That is no country for old men. The young
In one another's arms, birds in the trees
—Those dying generations—at their song,
The salmon-falls, the mackerel-crowded seas,

Fish, flesh, or fowl, commend all summer long
Whatever is begotten, born, and dies.
Caught in that sensual music all neglect
Monuments of unageing intellect.

II

An aged man is but a paltry thing,
A tattered coat upon a stick, unless
Soul clap its hands and sing, and louder sing
For every tatter in its mortal dress,
Nor is there singing school but studying
Monuments of its own magnificence;
And therefore I have sailed the seas and come
To the holy city of Byzantium.

III

O sages standing in God's holy fire
As in the gold mosaic of a wall,
Come from the holy fire, perne in a gyre,
And be the singing-masters of my soul.
Consume my heart away; sick with desire
And fastened to a dying animal
It knows not what it is; and gather me
Into the artifice of eternity.

IV

Once out of nature I shall never take
My bodily form from any natural thing,
But such a form as Grecian goldsmiths make
Of hammered gold and gold enamelling
To keep a drowsy Emperor awake;
Or set upon a golden bough to sing
To lords and ladies of Byzantium
Of what is past, or passing, or to come.

23

SHALL I COMPARE THEE TO A SUMMER'S DAY?

~

William Shakespeare

*P*edants like to cite the famous opening line of this sonnet to demonstrate the difference between "compare to" and "compare with." (The former has to do with metaphorical likening, the latter with a side-by-side comparison of objects from the same category.)

The sonneteers of Shakespeare's age inherited a packet of conventions from earlier Italian sonneteers, Francesco Petrarch being the most preeminent and the one whose name is used in the general adjective "Petrarchan," which refers to the rhetoric of love poems involving fanciful comparisons and fantastic exaggeration. But Sonnet XVIII (like Sonnet CXXX: "My mistress' eyes are nothing like the sun") could be called anti-Petrarchan, since it begins by *denying* the fitness of the comparison.

After a lighthearted opening, the poem sobers up somewhat with the hyperbolic claim of "eternal summer" for the addressee. The final claim—that the very verse we are reading is what confers eternal life—is a convention derived from Horace's *Odes*.

Shall I Compare Thee to a Summer's Day?

Shall I compare thee to a summer's day?
Thou art more lovely and more temperate:
Rough winds do shake the darling buds of May,
And summer's lease hath all too short a date;
Sometime too hot the eye of heaven shines,
And often is his gold complexion dimm'd;
And every fair from fair sometime declines,
By chance or nature's changing course untrimm'd:
But thy eternal summer shall not fade
Nor lose possession of that fair thou ow'st;
Nor shall Death brag thou wand'rest in his shade,
When in eternal lines to time thou grow'st;
    So long as men can breathe or eyes can see,
    So long lives this, and this gives life to thee.

24

LET ME NOT TO THE MARRIAGE
OF TRUE MINDS
~
William Shakespeare

"*T*rue" here means "faithful" and "constant."

Steadfastness and fidelity have been favorite themes of poets, who usually bemoan the fickle and laud the fixed (although in "Pied Beauty," above, p. 14, Hopkins praises what is freckled or fickle).

Shakespeare's Julius Caesar claims to be as "constant as the northern star"— that is, the Pole Star that seems not to move while all other stars revolve around it, and which can still be used in informal navigation.

Ink has been spilt over the reading of line 8, which probably refers to the star (whose elevation or celestial altitude can be known by instruments) but may refer to the bark (ship).

Let Me Not to the Marriage of True Minds

Let me not to the marriage of true minds
Admit impediments. Love is not love
Which alters when it alteration finds,
Or bends with the remover to remove.
O, no! it is an ever-fixed mark
That looks on tempests and is never shaken;
It is the star to every wand'ring bark,
Whose worth's unknown, although his height be taken.
Love's not Time's fool, though rosy lips and cheeks
Within his bending sickle's compass come;
Love alters not with his brief hours and weeks,
But bears it out even to the edge of doom.
    If this be error and upon me proved,
    I never writ, nor no man ever loved.

25

FEAR NO MORE THE HEAT O' THE SUN

~

William Shakespeare

*I*n the fourth act of *Cymbeline,* the princes Guiderius and Arviragus "say" this funeral song over the supposedly dead body of the supposed boy Fidele—really the living body of the woman Imogen. (Shakespeare's theater, which had no actresses, specialized in plots involving change or confusion of sex; there were, likewise, plenty of make-believe deaths.)

Fear No More the Heat o' the Sun

Fear no more the heat o' the sun,
   Nor the furious winter's rages;
Thou thy worldly task hast done,
   Home art gone, and ta'en thy wages:
Golden lads and girls all must,
As chimney-sweepers, come to dust.

Fear no more the frown o' the great;
   Thou art past the tyrant's stroke;
Care no more to clothe and eat;
   To thee the reed is as the oak:
The scepter, learning, physic, must
All follow this, and come to dust.

Fear no more the lightning flash,
   Nor the all-dreaded thunder stone;
Fear not slander, censure rash;
   Thou hast finished joy and moan:
All lovers young, all lovers must
Consign to thee, and come to dust.

No exorciser harm thee!
Nor no witchcraft charm thee!
Ghost unlaid forbear thee!
Nothing ill come near thee!
Quiet consummation have;
And renownéd be thy grave!

26

ODE TO A NIGHTINGALE
~
John Keats

K̲eats's "Ode on a Grecian Urn" (p. 101) is virtually selfless, hinting only at a vague plural first-person pronoun toward the end. "Ode to a Nightingale," on the other hand, smacks more of the Romantic concentration on the singular self, beginning "My heart aches" and ending "Do I wake or sleep?"

From the days of the Romantics to the present, poets have found birds—especially those that can sing or fly or both—to be apt symbols or "objective correlatives" of their own situation. Thomas Hardy, in a poem about poetry ("Shelley's Skylark"), even puts forward a pun linking "bird" and "bard." Whatever the cause, there are memorable bird poems by Wordsworth, Coleridge, Shelley, Poe, Hardy, Yeats, Stevens, and Eliot—but none stand higher than Keats's "Ode to a Nightingale," which is my candidate for *the* most beautiful poem in English.

Ode to a Nightingale

I

My heart aches, and a drowsy numbness pains
  My sense, as though of hemlock I had drunk,
Or emptied some dull opiate to the drains
  One minute past, and Lethe-wards had sunk:
'Tis not through envy of thy happy lot,
  But being too happy in thine happiness,—
    That thou, light-winged Dryad of the trees,
      In some melodious plot
Of beechen green, and shadows numberless,
  Singest of summer in full-throated ease.

II

O, for a draught of vintage! that hath been
  Cool'd a long age in the deep-delved earth,
Tasting of Flora and the country green,
  Dance, and Provençal song, and sunburnt mirth!

O for a beaker full of the warm South,
    Full of the true, the blushful Hippocrene,
      With beaded bubbles winking at the brim,
        And purple-stained mouth;
    That I might drink, and leave the world unseen,
      And with thee fade away into the forest dim:

III

Fade far away, dissolve, and quite forget
    What thou among the leaves hast never known,
The weariness, the fever, and the fret
    Here, where men sit and hear each other groan;
Where palsy shakes a few, sad, last gray hairs,
    Where youth grows pale, and specter-thin, dies;
Where but to think is to be full of sorrow
      And leaden-eyed despairs,
Where Beauty cannot keep her lustrous eyes,
    Or new Love pine at them beyond to-morrow.

IV

Away! away! for I will fly to thee,
    Not charioted by Bacchus and his pards,
But on the viewless wings of Poesy,
    Though the dull brain perplexes and retards:
Already with thee! tender is the night,
    And haply the Queen-Moon is on her throne,
      Cluster'd around by all her starry Fays;
        But here there is no light,
    Save what from heaven is with the breezes blown
      Through verdurous glooms and winding mossy ways.

V

I cannot see what flowers are at my feet,
    Nor what soft incense hangs upon the boughs,
But, in embalmed darkness, guess each sweet
    Wherewith the seasonable month endows
The grass, the thicket, and the fruit-tree wild;
    White hawthorn, and the pastoral eglantine;
      Fast fading violets cover'd up in leaves;
        And mid-May's eldest child,
    The coming musk-rose, full of dewy wine,
      The murmurous haunt of flies on summer eves.

VI

Darkling I listen; and, for many a time
　I have been half in love with easeful Death,
Call'd him soft names in many a mused rhyme,
　To take into the air my quiet breath;
Now more than ever seems it rich to die,
　To cease upon the midnight with no pain,
　　While thou art pouring forth thy soul abroad
　　　In such an ecstasy!
　Still wouldst thou sing, and I have ears in vain—
　　To thy high requiem become a sod.

VII

Thou wast not born for death, immortal Bird!
　No hungry generations tread thee down;
The voice I hear this passing night was heard
　In ancient days by emperor and clown:
Perhaps the self-same song that found a path
　Through the sad heart of Ruth, when, sick for home,
　　She stood in tears amid the alien corn;
　　　The same that oft-times hath
　Charm'd magic casements, opening on the foam
　Of perilous seas, in faery lands forlorn.

VIII

Forlorn! the very word is like a bell
　To toll me back from thee to my sole self!
Adieu! the fancy cannot cheat so well
　As she is fam'd to do, deceiving elf.
Adieu! adieu! thy plaintive anthem fades
　Past the near meadows, over the still stream,
　　Up the hill-side; and now 'tis buried deep
　　　In the next valley-glades:
　Was it a vision, or a waking dream?
　　Fled is that music:—Do I wake or sleep?

27

THE LOVE SONG OF
J. ALFRED PRUFROCK
~
T. S. Eliot

---

*A*lthough this poem is the last word in pooped modernist irony and sophistication, full of sardonic echoes, ragtime rhythms, and surrealist images, it was written by an uncommonly robust twenty-year-old.

The most salient discrepancy springs from the title itself, for the poem is hardly a love song—it is not a song and not really about love. It is, rather, a non-song about unlove, an affair of inversions and subversions. In the age of Theodore Roosevelt, the most representative literary creature is a milquetoast whose expression is a sort of black caricature of Arnold's "Dover Beach" (p. 20) or a Browning monologue, except that Prufrock's peregrinations seem centered on and addressed to himself more than to any imaginable interlocutor. Prufrock's outburst—"It is impossible to say just what I mean!"—shows the double-edged penknife of irony, for that surely is exactly what the poor man means.

As with Yeats's "The Lake Isle of Innisfree" (p. 182), the poem registers longing as a desire to *go:* Yeats's speaker says, "I will arise and go now, and go to Innisfree"; Eliot's says, "Let us go then, you and I . . . Let us go . . . Let us go . . ." but it is probable that neither speaker goes anywhere. The poems are sad soliloquies.

Early on, the poem likens fog to a cat: the first appearance of the feline imagery that became almost an obsession with Eliot, whose poems abound in tigers, jaguars, leopards, and, of course, those *practical cats* that generated heaps of posthumous success in the musical theater.

The Love Song of J. Alfred Prufrock

S'io credessi che mia risposta fosse
a persona che mai tornasse al mondo,
questa fiamma staria senza più scosse.
Ma per ciò che giammai di questo fondo
non tornò vivo alcun, s'i' odo il vero,
senza tema d'infamia ti rispondo.

Let us go then, you and I,
When the evening is spread out against the sky
Like a patient etherised upon a table;
Let us go, through certain half-deserted streets,
The muttering retreats
Of restless nights in one-night cheap hotels
And sawdust restaurants with oyster-shells:
Streets that follow like a tedious argument
Of insidious intent
To lead you to an overwhelming question . . .
Oh, do not ask, "What is it?"
Let us go and make our visit.

In the room the women come and go
Talking of Michelangelo.

The yellow fog that rubs its back upon the window-panes,
The yellow smoke that rubs its muzzle on the window-panes,
Licked its tongue into the corners of the evening,
Lingered upon the pools that stand in drains,
Let fall upon its back the soot that falls from chimneys,
Slipped by the terrace, made a sudden leap,
And seeing that it was a soft October night,
Curled once about the house, and fell asleep.

And indeed there will be time
For the yellow smoke that slides along the street
Rubbing its back upon the window-panes;
There will be time, there will be time
To prepare a face to meet the faces that you meet;
There will be time to murder and create,
And time for all the works and days of hands
That lift and drop a question on your plate;
Time for you and time for me,
And time yet for a hundred indecisions,
And for a hundred visions and revisions,
Before the taking of a toast and tea.

In the room the women come and go
Talking of Michelangelo.

And indeed there will be time
To wonder, "Do I dare?" and, "Do I dare?"
Time to turn back and descend the stair,
With a bald spot in the middle of my hair—
(They will say: "How his hair is growing thin!")
My morning coat, my collar mounting firmly to the chin,
My necktie rich and modest, but asserted by a simple pin—
(They will say: "But how his arms and legs are thin!")
Do I dare
Disturb the universe?
In a minute there is time
For decisions and revisions which a minute will reverse.

For I have known them all already, known them all—
Have known the evenings, mornings, afternoons,
I have measured out my life with coffee spoons;
I know the voices dying with a dying fall
Beneath the music from a farther room.
    So how should I presume?

And I have known the eyes already, known them all—
The eyes that fix you in a formulated phrase,
And when I am formulated, sprawling on a pin,
When I am pinned and wriggling on the wall,
Then how should I begin
To spit out all the butt-ends of my days and ways?
    And how should I presume?

And I have known the arms already, known them all—
Arms that are braceleted and white and bare
(But in the lamplight, downed with light brown hair!)
Is it perfume from a dress
That makes me so digress?
Arms that lie along a table, or wrap about a shawl.
    And should I then presume?
    And how should I begin?

        . . . . .
Shall I say, I have gone at dusk through narrow streets
And watched the smoke that rises from the pipes
Of lonely men in shirt-sleeves, leaning out of windows? . . .

I should have been a pair of ragged claws
Scuttling across the floors of silent seas.

. . . . .

And the afternoon, the evening, sleeps so peacefully!
Smoothed by long fingers,
Asleep . . . tired . . . or it malingers,
Stretched on the floor, here beside you and me.
Should I, after tea and cakes and ices,
Have the strength to force the moment to its crisis?
But though I have wept and fasted, wept and prayed,
Though I have seen my head (grown slightly bald) brought in upon a
    platter,
I am no prophet—and here's no great matter;
I have seen the moment of my greatness flicker,
And I have seen the eternal Footman hold my coat, and snicker,
And in short, I was afraid.

And would it have been worth it, after all,
After the cups, the marmalade, the tea,
Among the porcelain, among some talk of you and me,
Would it have been worth while,
To have bitten off the matter with a smile,
To have squeezed the universe into a ball
To roll it towards some overwhelming question,
To say: "I am Lazarus, come from the dead,
Come back to tell you all, I shall tell you all"—
If one, settling a pillow by her head,
    Should say: "That is not what I meant at all.
    That is not it, at all."

And would it have been worth it, after all,
Would it have been worth while,
After the sunsets and the dooryards and the sprinkled streets,
After the novels, after the teacups, after the skirts that trail along the
    floor—
And this, and so much more?—
It is impossible to say just what I mean!
But as if a magic lantern threw the nerves in patterns on a screen:
Would it have been worth while
If one, settling a pillow or throwing off a shawl,

And turning toward the window, should say:
   "That is not it at all,
   That is not what I meant, at all."
       . . . . .

No! I am not Prince Hamlet, nor was meant to be;
Am an attendant lord, one that will do
To swell a progress, start a scene or two,
Advise the prince; no doubt, an easy tool,
Deferential, glad to be of use,
Politic, cautious, and meticulous;
Full of high sentence, but a bit obtuse;
At times, indeed, almost ridiculous—
Almost, at times, the Fool.

I grow old . . . I grow old . . .
I shall wear the bottoms of my trousers rolled.

Shall I part my hair behind? Do I dare to eat a peach?
I shall wear white flannel trousers, and walk upon the beach.
I have heard the mermaids singing, each to each.

I do not think that they will sing to me.

I have seen them riding seaward on the waves
Combing the white hair of the waves blown back
When the wind blows the water white and black.

We have lingered in the chambers of the sea
By sea-girls wreathed with seaweed red and brown
Till human voices wake us, and we drown.

28

TO HELEN

~

Edgar Allan Poe

*P*oe's "To Helen" seems a conglomeration of imperfections that somehow, unaccountably—presto!—create a living and durable work of art, and arguably the greatest lyric poem ever written by an American. In terms of meter and rhyme, the stanzas don't match. The grammar of the second stanza, wherein "long wont" is a dangling modifier, is nearly illiterate; in the same stanza, the rhymes are of a kind that Poe castigated in others ("face" and "Greece" don't fully rhyme, and "roam" and "Rome" don't really rhyme at all. Identical sounds are not true rhymes.)

The personal reference is most indefinite, although Poe conceded that the subject was a young woman—Mrs. Jane Stith Stanard—who died when the poet was fifteen. The classical trappings are both allusive and elusive, as though the poet preferred vague suggestions to distinct registrations. Nobody has even satisfactorily explained "Nicéan"; and "Naiad" and "Psyche" are likewise indeterminate. Still, the poem is a gem. It was first drafted when the poet was fourteen, so that it seems likely that "To Helen," of all the poems in this book, had the youngest author.

The poem combines two fascinating themes: praise and homecoming, and it took a special reach of genius to liken the subject's beauty to the vessel that brings an Odysseus, say, home to his own native shore. The notion of home is then expanded to include the glory and grandeur of classical antiquity, and then—in yet another Olympic-class leap (Poe was a jumper)—extended still further to include the Holy Land (a term that preserves the basic consonant-pattern of "Helen").

To Helen

Helen, thy beauty is to me
　　Like those Nicéan barks of yore,
That gently, o'er a perfumed sea,
　　The weary, way-worn wanderer bore
　　To his own native shore.

On desperate seas long wont to roam,
    Thy hyacinth hair, thy classic face,
Thy Naiad airs have brought me home
    To the glory that was Greece,
And the grandeur that was Rome.

Lo! in yon brilliant window-niche
    How statue-like I see thee stand,
    The agate lamp within thy hand!
Ah, Psyche, from the regions which
    Are Holy-Land!

29

BECAUSE I COULD NOT STOP FOR DEATH

~

Emily Dickinson

*D*ickinson was only five years older than Mark Twain, and, although she has little in common with him, we might detect what the French would call a streak of Huckfinnishness in her persona-pose of Wise Child, with its wisdom and childishness, not to mention its idiosyncrasy of spelling and punctuation. And Death.

Edgar Allan Poe had kept up a Romantic concentration on the funereal that derived from the Graveyard and Gothic fashions of the eighteenth century, and Dickinson, a generation younger than Poe, came along just in time to witness a mass-movement in obituary poetry so widespread and so bathetically lugubrious that it became a joke. Mark Twain and others repeatedly made fun of the death poems of Julia A. Moore (1847–1920), the "Sweet Singer of Michigan," who appears disguised as the already dead Emmeline Grangerford in *Huckleberry Finn.*

But, of course, these jokes are things done on the way to a funeral that is not a joke. Dickinson shared also Huck Finn's courage and profundity, and, like Mark Twain, Ambrose Bierce, and others of their generation, used humor to accommodate the refrigerating horror of mortality.

This poem bravely seeks to naturalize and domesticate Death by personifying it as a civil gentleman, not so different from Walt Whitman's "lovely and soothing death" or even Keats's "easeful death." But all of these muting adjectives work because everybody knows in her and his bones that death is nothing but a brute beast.

Because I Could Not Stop for Death

Because I could not stop for Death—
He kindly stopped for me—
The Carriage held but just Ourselves—
And Immortality.

We slowly drove—He knew no haste
And I had put away
My labor and my leisure too,
For His Civility—

We passed the School, where Children strove
At Recess—in the Ring—
We passed the Fields of Gazing Grain—
We passed the Setting Sun—

Or rather—He passed Us—
The Dews drew quivering and chill—
For only Gossamer, my Gown—
My Tippet—only Tulle—

We paused before a House that seemed
A Swelling of the Ground—
The Roof was scarcely visible—
The Cornice—in the Ground—

Since then—'tis Centuries—and yet
Feels shorter than the Day
I first surmised the Horses' Heads
Were toward Eternity—

30

THE WINDHOVER

~

Gerard Manley Hopkins

---

*L*ike most of Hopkins's other poems—and like all four of his poems in this book—"The Windhover" was not published until 1918, nearly thirty years after the poet's death.

It is among the half-dozen great "bird poems" in this collection, all of which suggest that we use the subhuman realm of animals to symbolize the superhuman realm of abstractions and deities ("Hope" in Hardy's "The Darkling Thrush" and Zeus in Yeats's "Leda and the Swan," the latter of which presents some striking similarities to "The Windhover").

The poem, in every detail, is a striking study in dynamic contrasts, even in the punctuation. The first hyphen (in "king-/ dom") makes two words out of one; those in "dapple-dawn-drawn" make one word out of three. In the larger design, Christ is hyphenated with the smallest of the predatory birds. Even the first verb is contradictory: the poet did not literally "catch" the bird but figuratively "caught sight" (as in the contemporary expression, "Did you catch the news last night?").

Notice that the rarer dialect form "windhover" is much more vivid than "kestrel" (the common name for the creature), and, being truncated from the clumsy "windhoverer," seems to be a noun and verb at once: the thing *is* what it *does*. Notice also that Hopkins combines noun and verb forms in "the achieve of," wherein a dynamic verb takes the place of a static noun ("achievement").

"Buckle" means both "come together" and "fall apart," and in this usage is both imperative and declarative: economical grammar!

The usual representation of Christian theology finds its symbols in lamb and dove, but Hopkins here concentrates on a predator (which may seem villainous, as the kestrel is from the rodents' viewpoint in *Watership Down*) in the act of hunting. As it hovers, seeming to defy gravity and rebuff the wind, it is a prince of the kingdom of morning; as it collapses its wings and turns on them ("wimpling" means "rippling" and "turning"), it reflects the light of the rising sun. After the fantastic description of the bird in the first nine lines, Hopkins turns to the poem's addressee, "Christ our Lord," and asserts that His glory is a billion times that of the bird. And this is the British billion, which is 1,000,000,000,000, not just the relatively understated French and American billion (1,000,000,000). This Christ is "dangerous" (from *dominus,* "master") and a mounted warrior knight ("chevalier").

The comparison of Christ to a million-million predators is breathtaking enough, to be sure, but the last three lines are even more spectacular, for here the tone is lowered to the most modest things: a ploughshare polished to shining (and, like the bird, reflecting sunlight) as it precedes the plodding laborer down the furrow ("sillion"); and an all-but-dead ember in a fireplace. In imagery drawn from the Crucifixion ("gall" and "gash") and the Eucharist (gold-vermilion parallel to bread-wine, in turn parallel to flesh-blood), the ember sends out brilliant light.

The Windhover

To Christ Our Lord

I caught this morning morning's minion, king-
    dom of daylight's dauphin, dapple-dawn-drawn Falcon, in his riding
    Of the rolling level underneath him steady air, and striding
High there, how he rung upon the rein of a wimpling wing
In his ecstasy! then off, off forth on swing,
    As a skate's heel sweeps smooth on a bow-bend: the hurl and gliding
    Rebuffed the big wind. My heart in hiding
Stirred for a bird,—the achieve of, the mastery of the thing!

Brute beauty and valour and act, oh, air, pride, plume, here
    Buckle! AND the fire that breaks from thee then, a billion
Times told lovelier, more dangerous. O my chevalier!

    No wonder of it: shéer plód makes plough down sillion
Shine, and blue-bleak embers, ah my dear,
    Fall, gall themselves, and gash gold-vermilion.

31

ANTHEM FOR DOOMED YOUTH

~

Wilfred Owen

*P*aul Fussell's book *The Great War and Modern Memory* has shown that World War I came as a distinct and horrible shock to a Europe that had been relatively at peace for a hundred years. The new physics and chemistry produced weapons of unexampled ferocity and efficiency, and the utter horror of warfare could no longer be ignored or camouflaged as patriotic glory.

During the Boer War, twenty years before, Thomas Hardy had shown the inanity of the rhetoric of Tennyson's "The Charge of the Light Brigade." Hardy gave the plain facts:

> They throw in Drummer Hodge to rest,
> Uncoffined, just as found.

Owen and other poets of the Great War kept up the campaign of realism and honesty.

Owen was killed November 4, 1918—a week before the Armistice.

Anthem for Doomed Youth

What passing-bells for these who die as cattle?
— Only the monstrous anger of the guns.
Only the stuttering rifles' rapid rattle
Can patter out their hasty orisons.
No mockeries now for them; no prayers nor bells,
Nor any voice of mourning save the choirs,—
The shrill, demented choirs of wailing shells;
And bugles calling for them from sad shires.

What candles may be held to speed them all?
Not in the hands of boys but in their eyes
Shall shine the holy glimmers of goodbyes.
The pallor of girls' brows shall be their pall;
Their flowers the tenderness of patient minds,
And each slow dusk a drawing-down of blinds.

32

WHEN ICICLES HANG BY THE WALL

~

William Shakespeare

*T*wo songs are sung at the end of *Love's Labour's Lost,* one associated with "Ver, the Spring" and the cuckoo ("When daisies pied and violets blue") and this companion-piece, or complement, associated with "Hiems, Winter" and the owl.

As with much else in Shakespeare, the songs are infinitely better than they have to be, and some things that exceed necessity by a good measure also survive their original settings by a commensurate amount. It may seem easy to write a simple winter song, such as "Winter Wonderland" or "Jingle Bells," but it takes genius to fill the picture with specific and unforgettable sketches that create three-dimensional characters with maximal economy of means. Marian, or at least her nose "red and raw," has achieved immortality; and forever will "greasy Joan" be at her pot.

When Icicles Hang by the Wall

When icicles hang by the wall
And Dick the shepherd blows his nail
And Tom bears logs into the hall,
    And milk comes frozen home in pail.
When blood is nipped and ways be foul,
Then nightly sings the staring owl,
       Tu-who;
Tu-whit, tu-who: a merry note,
While greasy Joan doth keel the pot.

When all aloud the wind doth blow,
    And coughing drowns the parson's saw,
And birds sit brooding in the snow,
    And Marian's nose looks red and raw,

When roasted crabs hiss in the bowl,
Then nightly sings the staring owl,
      Tu-who;
Tu-whit, tu-who: a merry note
While greasy Joan doth keel the pot.

33

BATTER MY HEART, THREE-PERSONED GOD

~

John Donne

Donne's nineteen "Holy Sonnets," written around 1610–20, are in some ways a part and a culmination of a fashion in sonnet-writing that had been going on for about seventy-five years; but there are many ways in which a "holy sonnet" is a pronounced departure from fashion and convention.

As practiced by Wyatt, Surrey, Shakespeare, Sidney, and Spenser, the sonnet was relatively "unholy"; it was a secular love lyric that could become intensely erotic and also lightheartedly satirical. And it could exploit love's capacity for exaggeration and paradox, which is caricatured in some of Shakespeare's sonnets ("Shall I compare thee to a summer's day?" on page 48 and "My mistress' eyes are nothing like the sun" —both of which make fun of outlandish comparisons).

In his "Holy Sonnets," Donne lifted the level of love from secular to sacred, but he kept the dramatic emphasis on paradox (especially notable in the conclusion here: "I/ Except you enthrall me, never shall be free./ Nor ever chaste, except you ravish me"). He also kept much of the physical, erotic imagery from secular love lyrics; some readers may still find these paradoxes outlandish, for they ask God to divorce, imprison, and ravish the worshiper.

Donne was respected in his own day but was also considered an extremist and a needlessly difficult versifier. His reputation rose from moribundity during the middle third of this century.

This poem, by the way, was on J. Robert Oppenheimer's mind when he gave the name "Trinity" to the atomic bomb tests in 1945.

Batter My Heart, Three-Personed God

Batter my heart, three-personed God; for, you
As yet but knock, breathe, shine, and seek to mend;
That I may rise, and stand, o'erthrow me, and bend
Your force, to break, blow, burn, and make me new.
I, like an usurped town, to another due,

Labor to admit you, but oh, to no end,
Reason your viceroy in me, me should defend,
But is captived, and proves weak or untrue,
Yet dearly I love you, and would be loved fain,
But am betrothed unto your enemy,
Divorce me, untie, or break that knot again,
Take me to you, imprison me, for I
Except you enthrall me, never shall be free,
Nor ever chaste, except you ravish me.

34

LOVE

~

George Herbert

---

*A*lmost all of Herbert's poems are contained in one volume, called *The Temple,* published in the year of his death.

Like "The Collar" (p. 122), this "Love" (one of three poems Herbert wrote with that title) is a brightly colored, highly dramatized account of a conflict between a person and a principle—a man and a god. The temple is a scene of strife as well as a place of devotion.

The Love here seems to be a pagan Eros, but this Lord merges with the Christian God, the God who *is* Love.

Herbert's older brother Edward, known as Lord Herbert of Cherbury, was a mystical philosopher, and something of medieval "light" philosophy may persist in the notion that Love made eyes in the first place. Three centuries after the Herberts, Ezra Pound quoted the maxim *Ubi amor, ibi oculus:* where love is, there is the eye. Love, that is, is the organization of things that makes vision possible; and, as Hart Crane was to suggest, the company of love is visionary.

Love

Love bade me welcome; yet my soul drew back,
    Guilty of dust and sin.
But quick-eyed Love, observing me grow slack
    From my first entrance in,
Drew nearer to me, sweetly questioning
    If I lacked anything.

"A guest," I answered, "worthy to be here";
    Love said, "You shall be he."
"I, the unkind, ungrateful? Ah, my dear,
    I cannot look on Thee."
Love took my hand, and smiling did reply,
    "Who made the eyes but I?"

"Truth, Lord, but I have marred them; let my shame
  Go where it doth deserve."
"And know you not," says Love, "who bore the blame?"
  "My dear, then I will serve."
"You must sit down," says Love, "and taste My meat."
  So I did sit and eat.

35

ODE TO THE WEST WIND

~

Percy Bysshe Shelley

*P*salms, hymns, and odes flourish in cultures and ages distinguished by a
certain seriousness of attitude toward the world, literature, and humanity.
Odes are typically ambitious, dignified, and elevated, yet they should be
marked by musical charm as well ("ode" means "song").

Shelley wrote the "Ode to the West Wind" in Italy, one autumn two or
three years before his death. The poem soars on the loftiness of elementary
ideas: the elements, the seasons, the points of the compass. Normally these
entities are differential and separate us from nature and from each other. But
here, in a complex and passionate synthesis, Shelley connects the death of leaves
in autumn to the birth of seeds to come in the spring.

Another synthesis joins the poet himself to the world over which the wind
blows, and then he equates himself with the wind itself. Some may object to
the gushing outburst of

> I fall upon the thorns of life! I bleed!

but most of us can recognize the truth in Shelley's perception of the fact that,
when we encounter the world, we encounter ourselves also. Having made
himself and ourselves into waves, leaves, clouds, and lyres, it is easy for Shelley
to claim for himself the role of prophet. Some poems in this book are poems
about art, others are poems about poetry; this, in a unique sense, and among
all the other things it is about, is a poem about *itself.*

Ode to the West Wind

I

O wild West Wind, thou breath of Autumn's being,
Thou, from whose unseen presence the leaves dead
Are driven, like ghosts from an enchanter fleeing,

Yellow, and black, and pale, and hectic red,
Pestilence-stricken multitudes: O thou,
Who chariotest to their dark wintry bed

The winged seeds, where they lie cold and low,
Each like a corpse within its grave, until
Thine azure sister of the Spring shall blow

Her clarion o'er the dreaming earth, and fill
(Driving sweet buds like flocks to feed in air)
With living hues and odors plain and hill:

Wild Spirit, which art moving everywhere;
Destroyer and preserver; hear, oh, hear!

II

Thou on whose stream, mid the steep sky's commotion,
Loose clouds like earth's decaying leaves are shed,
Shook from the tangled boughs of Heaven and Ocean,

Angels of rain and lightning: there are spread
On the blue surface of thine aëry surge,
Like the bright hair uplifted from the head

Of some fierce Maenad, even from the dim verge
Of the horizon to the zenith's height,
The locks of the approaching storm. Thou dirge

Of the dying year, to which this closing night
Will be the dome of a vast sepulcher,
Vaulted with all thy congregated might

Of vapors, from whose solid atmosphere
Black rain, and fire, and hail will burst: oh, hear!

III

Thou who didst waken from his summer dreams
The blue Mediterranean, where he lay,
Lulled by the coil of his crystalline streams,

Beside a pumice isle in Baiae's bay,
And saw in sleep old palaces and towers
Quivering within the wave's intenser day,

All overgrown with azure moss and flowers
So sweet, the sense faints picturing them! Thou
For whose path the Atlantic's level powers

Cleave themselves into chasms, while far below
The sea-blooms and the oozy woods which wear
The sapless foliage of the ocean, know

Thy voice, and suddenly grow gray with fear,
And tremble and despoil themselves: oh, hear!

IV

If I were a dead leaf thou mightest bear;
If I were a swift cloud to fly with thee;
A wave to pant beneath thy power, and share

The impulse of thy strength, only less free
Than thou, O uncontrollable! If even
I were as in my boyhood, and could be

The comrade of thy wanderings over Heaven,
As then, when to outstrip thy skiey speed
Scarce seemed a vision; I would ne'er have striven

As thus with thee in prayer in my sore need.
Oh, lift me as a wave, a leaf, a cloud!
I fall upon the thorns of life! I bleed!

A heavy weight of hours has chained and bowed
One too like thee: tameless, and swift, and proud.

V

Make me thy lyre, even as the forest is:
What if my leaves are falling like its own!
The tumult of thy mighty harmonies

Will take from both a deep, autumnal tone,
Sweet though in sadness. Be thou, Spirit fierce,
My spirit! Be thou me, impetuous one!

Drive my dead thoughts over the universe
Like withered leaves to quicken a new birth!
And, by the incantation of this verse,

Scatter, as from an unextinguished hearth
Ashes and sparks, my words among mankind!
Be through my lips to unawakened earth

The trumpet of a prophecy! O, Wind,
If Winter comes, can Spring be far behind?

36

GOD'S GRANDEUR

~

Gerard Manley Hopkins

As we saw with Hopkins's "Pied Beauty" (p. 14), a good deal of his practice as a poet was devoted to living up to the motto of the Jesuit order to which he belonged: *Ad maiorem Dei gloriam,* "To the greater glory of God."

The conventional expressions of God's grandeur take the form of exaggeration; God is a loving parent, shepherd, or landlord, omnipotent, infinite, and eternal. But Hopkins here chooses a humbler path. After using the surprising physical figure "charged" (probably like a liquid being "charged" with gas but also, possibly, with electrical meanings), Hopkins resorts to domestic artifacts for his likenesses: foil (gold foil, in this case, but not deeply different from the light-show of tin or aluminum foil) and oil (probably olive oil, "crushed" as in a press). That God's grandeur can be thus expressed in modest terms is in itself testimony to the way that grandeur *charges* everything in the world.

In this poem, as well as in "Pied Beauty" and "The Windhover" (p. 64), Hopkins rhymes the flat "thing(s)" with the soaring "wing(s)," as though in a scale-model practical demonstration of how God's grandeur can suffuse the simplest words and verbal effects.

God's Grandeur

The world is charged with the grandeur of God.
    It will flame out, like shining from shook foil;
    It gathers to a greatness, like the ooze of oil
Crushed. Why do men then now not reck his rod?
Generations have trod, have trod, have trod;
    And all is seared with trade; bleared, smeared with toil;
    And wears man's smudge and shares man's smell: the soil
Is bare now, nor can foot feel, being shod.

And for all this, nature is never spent;
    There lives the dearest freshness deep down things;
And though the last lights off the black West went
    Oh, morning, at the brown brink eastward, springs—
Because the Holy Ghost over the bent
    World broods with warm breast and with ah! bright wings.

37

DO NOT GO GENTLE INTO THAT GOOD NIGHT

~

Dylan Thomas

Many readers have come to regard Dylan Thomas as the greatest poet born in the British Isles in the twentieth century.

A comparison of "Do Not Go Gentle into That Good Night" with the earlier poem "A Refusal to Mourn the Death, by Fire, of a Child in London" will show that Thomas, although he died before his fortieth birthday, had time, in more than twenty years of mature writing, to progress, as Yeats and Eliot had done before him, from the more complex to the simple.

This poem originated as an address to the poet's dying father. The usual Christian pieties of an acquiescent death and peaceful rest after death are shoved aside in favor of an ungentle rage.

The ornate and obsessive verse form called villanelle began as a fairly trivial expression of love's ecstasy; but in some applications, such as those by Thomas Hardy, Edwin Arlington Robinson, and William Empson, the villanelle had deepened and darkened. Thomas's is surely the finest villanelle ever written as well as one of the finest poems of the twentieth century in *any* form.

Do Not Go Gentle into That Good Night

Do not go gentle into that good night,
Old age should burn and rave at close of day;
Rage, rage against the dying of the light.

Though wise men at their end know dark is right,
Because their words had forked no lightning they
Do not go gentle into that good night.

Good men, the last wave by, crying how bright
Their frail deeds might have danced in a green bay,
Rage, rage against the dying of the light.

Wild men who caught and sang the sun in flight,
And learn, too late, they grieved it on its way,
Do not go gentle into that good night.

Grave men, near death, who see with blinding sight
Blind eyes could blaze like meteors and be gay,
Rage, rage against the dying of the light.

And you, my father, there on the sad height,
Curse, bless, me now with your fierce tears, I pray,
Do not go gentle into that good night.
Rage, rage against the dying of the light.

38

WESTERN WIND

~

Anonymous

Since the fine poet and editor John Frederick Nims has given the name *Western Wind* to a most useful and entertaining anthology of poetry, it seems fitting here to quote his prose paraphrase of what is probably the oldest poem in this book:

> Characteristic of the coming of spring in Europe is the fact that prevailing winds are from the west; with them comes a marked increase of rainfall, though the spring rains tend to be gentle. I look forward with impatience to its coming, because at that time circumstances will be such that I will be reunited with the person I love and be given an opportunity to express that love in the normal human way.

Needless to say, Nims shows how his wittily bureaucratic paraphrase is inferior to the little poem, in which the elements are so physically present that the poet "addresses the wind as if it were alive."

Western Wind

Western wind, when wilt thou blow?
The small rain down can rain.
Christ, if my love were in my arms,
And I in my bed again!

39

THE LOVER SHOWETH HOW HE IS FORSAKEN OF SUCH AS HE SOMETIME ENJOYED

~

Sir Thomas Wyatt

Wyatt is the earliest named poet represented in this volume, and that is a small but apt tribute to the first poet to use both the terza rima and the ottava rima stanzas in English and one of the first, if not the very first, to write sonnets.

Many of Wyatt's poems are translations, but this one (which employs the stanza called rhyme royal) is original. In its paradoxes and complexities we may see the precursors of Metaphysical poetry that was to flourish almost a century later.

Even after almost five hundred years, we can still understand the meaning and the sound of many of Wyatt's lines:

> And sóftly sáid, "Dear héart, how líke you thís?"

Other lines, however, do not yield so easily, and we are not sure of the grammatical, prosodic, or musical principles that Wyatt was using; the effect remains bewitching, as in the beautiful but eccentric lines

> But all is turned thorough my gentleness
> Into a strange fashion of forsaking.

Those who, like me, associate "newfangled" with the idiom of George "Gabby" Hayes ("Y'er durn tootin', Hoppy, I don't want nothin' to do with these here newfangled horseless carriages") will be refreshingly surprised to see "newfangleness" in a poem from the early sixteenth century.

The Lover Showeth How He Is Forsaken of Such as He Sometime Enjoyed

They flee from me that sometime did me seek
With naked foot stalking in my chamber.
I have seen them gentle, tame, and meek
That now are wild and do not remember

That sometime they put themself in danger
To take bread at my hand; and now they range
Busily seeking with a continual change.

Thanked be fortune it hath been otherwise
Twenty times better, but once in special,
In thin array after a pleasant guise,
When her loose gown from her shoulders did fall
And she me caught in her arms long and small,
Therewithal sweetly did me kiss
And softly said, "Dear heart, how like you this?"

It was no dream: I lay broad waking.
But all is turned thorough my gentleness
Into a strange fashion of forsaking.
And I have leave to go of her goodness
And she also to use newfangleness.
But since that I so kindly am served
I would fain know what she hath deserved.

40

THE GOOD-MORROW

~

John Donne

Most love poems deal either with the insipidly satisfied or the cornily anguished. "The Good-Morrow," which Donne wrote before he became a celebrated preacher, is a convincing expression of satisfied love without the insipidity or smugness that threatens to wreck such a poem.

Donne, who was prodigiously learned in all sorts of disciplines, had a unique genius for applying images and terms from history, geography, and cartography to the private and intimate realm of love. Some later commentators doubted the wisdom of using intellectual arguments and materials in love poetry. John Dryden said that Donne "affects the metaphysics . . . and perplexes the minds of the fair sex with nice speculations of philosophy, when he should engage their hearts, and entertain them with the softnesses of love." Samuel Johnson said of the whole Metaphysical school, "Their courtship was void of fondness and their lamentation of sorrow. Their wish was only to say what they hoped had been never said before." In our time, on the other hand, T. S. Eliot has praised Donne and his followers for preserving a unity of sensibility missing in Dryden, say, who so sharply separated mind from heart. For Donne, mind and heart were one, and love could employ the idiom of physics, and vice versa.

The Good-Morrow

I wonder by my troth, what thou, and I
    Did, till we loved? were we not weaned till then,
  But sucked on country pleasures, childishly?
    Or snorted we in the seven sleepers' den?
'Twas so; but this, all pleasures fancies be.
If ever any beauty I did see,
Which I desired, and got, 'twas but a dream of thee.

And now good-morrow to our waking souls,
    Which watch not one another out of fear;
For love, all love of other sights controls,

And makes one little room, an every where.
Let sea-discoverers to new worlds have gone,
Let maps to others, worlds on worlds have shown,
Let us possess one world, each hath one, and is one.

My face in thine eye, thine in mine appears,
  And true plain hearts do in the faces rest,
Where can we find two better hemispheres
  Without sharp north, without declining west?
What ever dies, was not mixed equally;
If our two loves be one, or, thou and I
Love so alike, that none do slacken, none can die.

41

DELIGHT IN DISORDER

~

Robert Herrick

---

*P*oetry is a working model of a system of ordered patterns, and as such is a fine medium for the promotion of order and the punishment of disorder. It has been noticed that the end of a literary work normally involves an achievement of some sort of ordered resolution, whether matrimony as in comedy or the slaughter of whole houses as in tragedy.

It was clever of Herrick, therefore, to see that poetry could also be used to praise disorder. Like his master Ben Jonson, Herrick was a classicist, but in this poem he departs from his master's love of order and also his orderly verse. In praising disorder (a praise echoed in our time by the French critic Roland Barthes), Herrick practices what he preaches by exhibiting a modest degree of disorder in rhetoric, logic, grammar, and versification.

Delight in Disorder

A sweet disorder in the dress
Kindles in clothes a wantonness.
A lawn about the shoulders thrown
Into a fine distractión;
An erring lace, which here and there
Enthralls the crimson stomacher;
A cuff neglectful, and thereby
Ribbons to flow confusedly;
A winning wave, deserving note,
In the tempestuous petticoat;
A careless shoestring, in whose tie
I see a wild civility;
Do more bewitch me than when art
Is too precise in every part.

42

I WANDERED LONELY
AS A CLOUD

~

William Wordsworth

A doctrine of simplehearted harmony with rural nature was a foundation stone of Romanticism, and Wordsworth was the most eloquent spokesman of that belief.

One could conceivably force complications into such poetry, because it is profound, but the essential feeling is as simple as it is familiar.

I Wandered Lonely as a Cloud

I wandered lonely as a cloud
That floats on high o'er vales and hills,
When all at once I saw a crowd,
A host, of golden daffodils;
Beside the lake, beneath the trees,
Fluttering and dancing in the breeze.

Continuous as the stars that shine
And twinkle on the milky way,
They stretched in never-ending line
Along the margin of a bay:
Ten thousand saw I at a glance,
Tossing their heads in sprightly dance.

The waves beside them danced; but they
Out-did the sparkling waves in glee:
A poet could not but be gay,
In such a jocund company:
I gazed—and gazed—but little thought
What wealth the show to me had brought:

For oft, when on my couch I lie
In vacant or in pensive mood,
They flash upon that inward eye
Which is the bliss of solitude;
And then my heart with pleasure fills,
And dances with the daffodils.

43

MY LAST DUCHESS

~

Robert Browning

*R*obert Browning wrote many dramatic monologues, but this one rhymes, whereas the others tend to be in blank verse; and here the speaker reaches out, as it were, to speak the title, so that the poem's orbit goes from "My" to "me," an apt index of the speaker's character as a man so self-centered that he has ordered the murder of his earlier wife, just because she did not venerate him with quite the total devotion he demanded.

Now, negotiating with an envoy from a neighboring count who has an eligible daughter, the duke is masterly and wily but rather nervous. Three times he falls into what linguists call "overcorrection," saying "but I," "nine-hundred-years-old," and "such an one"—all tipoffs that he is being a shade too careful, lest he let the cat out of the bag (the cat's name is Murder).

It has been observed that the duke's admiration for a bronze of Neptune Taming a Sea Horse shows his dedication to mastery and domination; just as he tried to dominate the earlier duchess, he is trying now to monopolize and dominate his negotiations with the envoy. It has also been observed that the title phrase "last duchess" may betray the duke's coming destiny, since "last" can mean "most recent" but also "final." The duke thinks he means the former, but, unless the envoy is a dodo, the latter is more likely in this instance.

And now you can answer half of the famous English department exam question: Name two literary works in which an Italian duchess is offered fruit. (The other is of Malfi, and the fruit is the apricot.)

My Last Duchess

That's my last Duchess painted on the wall,
Looking as if she were alive. I call
That piece a wonder, now: Frà Pandolf's hands
Worked busily a day, and there she stands.
Will't please you sit and look at her? I said
"Frà Pandolf" by design, for never read
Strangers like you that pictured countenance,
The depth and passion of its earnest glance,
But to myself they turned (since none puts by

The curtain I have drawn for you, but I)
And seemed as they would ask me, if they durst,
How such a glance came there; so, not the first
Are you to turn and ask thus. Sir, 't was not
Her husband's presence only, called that spot
Of joy into the Duchess' cheek: perhaps
Frà Pandolf chanced to say "Her mantle laps
Over my lady's wrist too much," or "Paint
Must never hope to reproduce the faint
Half-flush that dies along her throat": such stuff
Was courtesy, she thought, and cause enough
For calling up that spot of joy. She had
A heart—how shall I say?—too soon made glad,
Too easily impressed; she liked whate'er
She looked on, and her looks went everywhere.
Sir, 't was all one! My favor at her breast,
The dropping of the daylight in the West,
The bough of cherries some officious fool
Broke in the orchard for her, the white mule
She rode with round the terrace—all and each
Would draw from her alike the approving speech,
Or blush, at least. She thanked men,—good! but thanked
Somehow—I know not how—as if she ranked
My gift of a nine-hundred-years-old name
With anybody's gift. Who'd stoop to blame
This sort of trifling? Even had you skill
In speech—(which I have not)—to make your will
Quite clear to such an one, and say, "Just this
Or that in you disgusts me; here you miss,
Or there exceed the mark"—and if she let
Herself be lessoned so, nor plainly set
Her wits to yours, forsooth, and made excuse,
—E'en then would be some stooping; and I choose
Never to stoop. Oh sir, she smiled, no doubt,
Whene'er I passed her; but who passed without
Much the same smile? This grew; I gave comands;
Then all smiles stopped together. There she stands
As if alive. Will't please you rise? We'll meet
The company below, then. I repeat,
The Count your master's known munificence
Is ample warrant that no just pretense
Of mine for dowry will be disallowed;

Though his fair daughter's self, as I avowed
At starting, is my object. Nay, we'll go
Together down, sir. Notice Neptune, though,
Taming a sea horse, thought a rarity,
Which Claus of Innsbruck cast in bronze for me!

44

SPRING AND FALL

~

Gerard Manley Hopkins

Of the four poems by Hopkins in this collection, "Spring and Fall" may be both the darkest and the most modern. It is certainly sober and static in comparison with the ecstatic celebrations in "Pied Beauty" (p. 14), "The Windhover" (p. 64), and "God's Grandeur" (p. 77). What seems peculiarly modern is the way the poem converts something physical (changing seasons) into something not only symbolic (the Fall) but also personally psychological, almost psychoanalytic, in that the child mourns for herself.

There are other modern qualities here. The title probes a certain mortal weakness in language itself, whereby "spring" can be a season and also a machine and a source of water and, by simple extension, any source, here, ironically, Sorrow's. The title also plays on the implicit possibility that what seems to be two nouns ("spring" and "fall") may also be two imperative verbs.

Hopkins lived at a time when speakers of English were anxious to rid their speech of foreign elements and adopt native locutions; this was when "popular antiquities" and "preface" became "folklore" and "foreword." Here Hopkins uses only words of Germanic extraction (the name "Margaret" is the sole exception) and the Germanic "sprung" rhythm that counts only stressed syllables. He also makes up new words like "wanwood" and "leafmeal" on a Germanic basis—all with the effect of strangeness but also of undeniable originality, authenticity, and sincerity.

Spring and Fall

to a young child

Márgarét, áre you gríeving
Over Goldengrove unleaving?
Leáves líke the things of man, you
With your fresh thoughts care for, can you?
Ah! ás the heart grows older
It will come to such sights colder
By and by, nor spare a sigh

Though worlds of wanwood leafmeal lie;
And yet you will weep and know why.
Now no matter, child, the name:
Sórrow's spríngs áre the same.
Nor mouth had, no nor mind, expressed
What heart heard of, ghost guessed:
It ís the blight man was born for,
It is Margaret you mourn for.

45

LEDA AND THE SWAN

~

William Butler Yeats

---

*L*ike Gerard Manley Hopkins's "The Windhover" (p.64), Yeats's "Leda and the Swan" is a sonnet in which a dangerous bird somehow stands for a god. Even the vocabulary is similar: Hopkins had written of the *"mastery* of the thing" and

> *Brute* beauty and valour and act, oh, *air,* pride, plume here
> Buckle!

And Yeats writes:

> So *mastered* by the *brute* blood of the *air.* . . .

Hopkins's poem was published in 1918; Yeats's was written in 1924. It is probable that Yeats read Hopkins; the two had met briefly a few years before Hopkins's death in 1889.

Yeats here hyphenates the two main kinds of sonnet; out of the Italian (*abba abba cde cde*) and English (*abab cdcd efef gg*) designs, he forges a new combination that may parallel the violent combining of divine, human, and animal: *abab cdcd efgefg.* He also inverts the usual question-and-answer format (used in his "September 1913") to a turbulent statement-question-statement-question design.

This is a rather mannered poem about a Renaissance painting (by someone of the school of Michelangelo) of an antiquated myth sometimes invoked to explain the origins of the Trojan War. Leda gave birth to Castor and Pollux (the Twins or Gemini, in whose sign Yeats was born on June 13), as well as to Helen and Clytemnestra, sisters who married the brothers Menelaus and Agamemnon, respectively, the latter of whom was murdered by his wife.

Leda and the Swan

A sudden blow: the great wings beating still
Above the staggering girl, her thighs caressed
By the dark webs, her nape caught in his bill,
He holds her helpless breast upon his breast.

How can those terrified vague fingers push
The feathered glory from her loosening thighs?
And how can body, laid in that white rush,
But feel the strange heart beating where it lies?

A shudder in the loins engenders there
The broken wall, the burning roof and tower
And Agamemnon dead.
                  Being so caught up,
So mastered by the brute blood of the air,
Did she put on his knowledge with his power
Before the indifferent beak could let her drop?

46

THE RIVER-MERCHANT'S WIFE: A LETTER

~

Ezra Pound

This poem demonstrates the folly of direct biographical criticism. It is, as any intelligent reader can detect in a second, a passionate and personal love poem, addressed to the beloved with no ambiguity. And yet it is by no means the direct utterance of the author in his contingent circumstance: "he" (so to speak) was a thirty-year-old American male living in London in 1915; he had never been to China and did not know Chinese very well (he relied on the notes of others, who likewise may not have been experts). Even so, in the imagined epistolary words of a teenage Chinese woman living on the other side of the world a thousand years earlier, Pound found the ideal expression of wedded bliss (he had himself gotten married a year earlier and exchanged hundreds of letters with his wife Dorothy).

Maybe because of his very amateurishness as a sinologist (abetted by genius and exuberance), Pound simplified the subtle idiom and style of Li Po's ("Rihaku" 's) verse to a flat and rather commercial prose (the addressee is a merchant, after all) concentrating on visual images of objects with primary colors (blue plums, yellow butterflies) like a woodblock print.

Pound was living with William Butler Yeats during the winters of 1913–14, 1914–15, and 1915–16, and borrowing much from Yeats (and lending as well). It seems probable that the end of this letter—three foreign syllables constituting an exotic place name—is indebted to the end of Yeats's "In the Seven Woods" (1903): "A cloudy quiver over Parc-na-Lee."

The River-Merchant's Wife: A Letter

While my hair was still cut straight across my forehead
I played about the front gate, pulling flowers.
You came by on bamboo stilts, playing horse,
You walked about my seat, playing with blue plums.
And we went on living in the village of Chokan:
Two small people, without dislike or suspicion.

At fourteen I married My Lord you.
I never laughed, being bashful.
Lowering my head, I looked at the wall.
Called to, a thousand times, I never looked back.

At fifteen I stopped scowling,
I desired my dust to be mingled with yours
Forever and forever and forever.
Why should I climb the look out?

At sixteen you departed,
You went into far Ku-to-yen, by the river of swirling eddies,
And you have been gone five months.
The monkeys make sorrowful noise overhead.
You dragged your feet when you went out.
By the gate now, the moss is grown, the different mosses,
Too deep to clear them away!
The leaves fall early this autumn, in wind.
The paired butterflies are already yellow with August
Over the grass in the West garden;
They hurt me. I grow older.
If you are coming down through the narrows of the river Kiang,
Please let me know beforehand,
And I will come out to meet you
                    As far as Cho-fu-Sa.

                                        By Rihaku

47

GO, LOVELY ROSE

~

Edmund Waller

An "envoy" is, literally, somebody *sent* to a foreign government on a diplomatic mission, and an "invoice" is a list of things *sent*. Likewise, an "envoy" is the name of a *sending* poem that acts as a go-between for a poet who for some reason cannot address his or her love directly.

Here the symbolic rose is economically used as a tribute and also as an example of what can happen to wasted beauty, much like the rose-buds in Herrick's "To the Virgins, to Make Much of Time" (p. 26) and the flower in Gray's "Elegy Written in a Country Churchyard" that is "born to blush unseen,/ And waste its sweetness on the desert air" (p. 40).

Waller's contemporary Henry Lawes set "Go, Lovely Rose" to music, and both artists survive in our century in the so-called *Envoi* of Ezra Pound's *Hugh Selwyn Mauberley:*

> Go, dumb-born book,
> Tell her that sang me once that song of Lawes. . . .
> Tell her that goes
> With song upon her lips
> But sings not out the song, nor knows
> The maker of it, some other mouth,
> May be as fair as hers,
> Might, in new ages, gain her worshipers,
> When our two dusts with Waller's shall be laid,
> Siftings on siftings in oblivion,
> Till change hath broken down
> All things save Beauty alone.

Go, Lovely Rose

> Go, lovely rose,
> Tell her that wastes her time and me
> That now she knows,
> When I resemble her to thee,
> How sweet and fair she seems to be.

Tell her that's young
And shuns to have her graces spied,
    That hadst thou sprung
In deserts where no men abide,
Thou must have uncommended died.

    Small is the worth
Of beauty from the light retired:
    Bid her come forth,
Suffer herself to be desired,
And not blush so to be admired.

    Then die, that she
The common fate of all things rare
    May read in thee,
How small a part of time they share
That are so wondrous sweet and fair.

48

THE RETREAT

~

Henry Vaughan

---

*H*enry Vaughan is the only poet represented in this book who was a twin; his brother Thomas (1622–66) was also a writer, though less well known for poetry than for alchemical prose.

With a mildly "metaphysical" species of wit typical of the poetry of the mid-seventeenth century, Vaughan here plays on both the common senses of "retreat" (a movement backward as well as a place of shelter and meditation). There is also a structure of play on the "re-" prefix (meaning both "back" and "again") in the title and the last word. (Much the same sort of verbal play is present in Milton's *Paradise Regained,* the last word of which is "returned.") In expressing a desire to return to childhood's angelic innocence, the poet returns to a certain childlike play on words and figures.

The Retreat

Happy those early days! when I
Shined in my angel-infancy.
Before I understood this place
Appointed for my second race,
Or taught my soul to fancy ought
But a white, celestial thought,
When yet I had not walked above
A mile or two, from my first love,
And looking back (at that short space)
Could see a glimpse of his bright face;
When on some *gilded cloud,* or *flower*
My gazing soul would dwell an hour,
And in those weaker glories spy
Some shadows of eternity;
Before I taught my tongue to wound
My conscience with a sinful sound,
Or had the black art to dispense
A sev'ral sin to ev'ry sense,

But felt through all this fleshly dress
Bright *shoots* of everlastingness.
   O how I long to travel back
And tread again that ancient track!
That I might once more reach that plain,
Where first I left my glorious train,
From whence th' inlightened spirit sees
That shady city of palm trees;
But (ah!) my soul with too much stay
Is drunk, and staggers in the way.
Some men a forward motion love,
But I by backward steps would move,
And when this dust falls to the urn
In that state I came return.

49

ODE ON A GRECIAN URN

~

John Keats

Keats lived at the apex of the Romantic Age, and his fate and work have both been considered as thoroughly typical of the spirit of Romanticism. It seems, however, that Keats's "Ode to a Nightingale" (p. 52) is the *most* Romantic of his odes; "Ode on a Grecian Urn" seems closer to the spirit of Classicism. The subject is an artifact from classical antiquity, and Keats's handling of the subject has an impersonal quality, reflected in the structural poise of the poem.

From beginning to end, the poem personifies the urn—first as bride, child, and historian, finally as a speaker with a strange message. Thanks to some confusion as to punctuation, it is unclear whether the urn says all of the last two lines or just "Beauty is truth, truth beauty."

Ode on a Grecian Urn

Thou still unravished bride of quietness,
   Thou foster-child of silence and slow time,
Sylvan historian, who canst thus express
   A flowery tale more sweetly than our rhyme:
What leaf-fringed legend haunts about thy shape
   Of deities or mortals, or of both,
      In Tempe or the dales of Arcady?
   What men or gods are these? What maidens loth?
What mad pursuit? What struggle to escape?
      What pipes and timbrels? What wild ecstasy?

Heard melodies are sweet, but those unheard
   Are sweeter; therefore, ye soft pipes, play on;
Not to the sensual ear, but, more endeared,
   Pipe to the spirit ditties of no tone:
Fair youth, beneath the trees, thou canst not leave
   Thy song, nor ever can those trees be bare;
   Bold Lover, never, never canst thou kiss,

Though winning near the goal—yet, do not grieve;
   She cannot fade, though thou hast not thy bliss,
For ever wilt thou love, and she be fair!

Ah, happy, happy boughs! that cannot shed
   Your leaves, nor ever bid the Spring adieu;
And, happy melodist, unwearíed,
   For ever piping songs for ever new;
More happy love! more happy, happy love!
   For ever warm and still to be enjoyed,
      For ever panting, and for ever young;
All breathing human passion far above,
   That leaves a heart high-sorrowful and cloyed,
      A burning forehead, and a parching tongue.

Who are these coming to the sacrifice?
   To what green altar, O mysterious priest,
Lead'st thou that heifer lowing at the skies,
   And all her silken flanks with garlands drest?
What little town by river or sea shore,
   Or mountain-built with peaceful citadel,
      Is emptied of this folk, this pious morn?
And, little town, thy streets for evermore
   Will silent be; and not a soul to tell
      Why thou art desolate, can e'er return.

O Attic shape! Fair attitude! with brede
   Of marble men and maidens overwrought,
With forest branches and the trodden weed;
   Thou, silent form, dost tease us out of thought
As doth Eternity: Cold Pastoral!
   When old age shall this generation waste,
      Thou shalt remain, in midst of other woe
Than ours, a friend to man, to whom thou say'st,
Beauty is truth, truth beauty,—that is all
   Ye know on earth, and all ye need to know.

50

LONDON

~

William Blake

---

*L*ike "The Tyger" (poem 1, p. 5 above), "London" appeared first in Blake's *Songs of Experience* (1794). It is very much a *song*, although not so liltingly lyrical as some songs, and very much about modern urban *experience*.

"The Tyger" contains no "I" and no statements: it is all questions asked by an unspecified speaker, ourselves as much as Blake. But "London" is about an "I" and is all statements made by the speaker in direct passionate response to a common experience, walking in a city and looking at faces.

Blake painstakingly fits his poem into a physical world that anybody can relate to, and he draws his passionate responses from everybody's ordinary fears and desires.

At the same time, Blake forges a strikingly original idiom that seems to foreshadow surrealist combinations of sensory images. Blake does not deal in abstractions or generalities. He does not loftily indict Prostitution or Disease, he presents a youthful Harlot; instead of airily discussing his concern over Child Labor, he lets us hear the Chimney-sweeper's cry. In the first half of the poem, some abstractions are mentioned: weakness, woe, fear; but in the second half there is nothing but physical realities, combined in extraordinary images of pity and terror.

London

I wander thro' each charter'd street,
Near where the charter'd Thames does flow.
And mark in every face I meet
Marks of weakness, marks of woe.

In every cry of every Man,
In every Infants cry of fear,
In every voice: in every ban,
The mind-forg'd manacles I hear

How the Chimney-sweepers cry
Every blackning Church appalls,
And the hapless Soldiers sigh,
Runs in blood down Palace walls

But most thro' midnight streets I hear
How the youthful Harlots curse
Blasts the new-born Infants tear
And blights with plagues the Marriage hearse

51

AND DID THOSE FEET

~

William Blake

*F*or British readers probably and American readers possibly, these words will be as familiar with a musical setting as without, a condition that is true of only one other poem in this book, Ben Jonson's "Song: To Celia" ("Drink to me only with thine eyes") (p. 121). "Jerusalem" is the title usually given to this hymn.

Some who saw the movie *Chariots of Fire* did not wonder much about the title because they did not know where it came from; some did wonder because they did know. Amateur track competition, even at the Olympic Games altitude, involves neither chariots nor fire.

Even so, Blake's words are very likely the most inspiriting ever written by an Englishman for Englishmen. A grand tradition of rugged struggle in politics and religion extends from John Milton and John Bunyan in the seventeenth century, through Blake and Wordsworth in the eighteenth and nineteenth, down to our own time in writers as diverse as W. B. Yeats and Joyce Cary.

And Did Those Feet

And did those feet in ancient time
Walk upon England's mountains green?
And was the holy Lamb of God
On England's pleasant pastures seen?

And did the Countenance Divine
Shine forth upon our clouded hills?
And was Jerusalem builded here,
Among these dark Satanic Mills?

Bring me my Bow of burning gold:
Bring me my Arrows of desire:
Bring me my Spear: O clouds unfold!
Bring me my Chariot of fire!

I will not cease from Mental Fight,
Nor shall my Sword sleep in my hand,
Till we have built Jerusalem
In England's green & pleasant Land.

52

COMPOSED UPON WESTMINSTER BRIDGE, SEPTEMBER 3, 1802

~

William Wordsworth

---

*A*nyone who regards Wordsworth as a vague and dreamy Romantic poet of rustic nature may be surprised by the unusual specificity of the title "Composed upon Westminster Bridge, September 3, 1802" and by the unusual subject: the majesty and splendor of a city in the early morning.

According to Wordsworth's sister Dorothy, the actual experience took place on July 31, 1802, and not September 3. In any event, the poem is poised on many thresholds in time and space: the beginning of a month and a century, the end of summer and the beginning of autumn, all seen from a special bridge leading to the area of Westminster Abbey and the Houses of Parliament. The part of London known particularly as "the City" is the financial district, a square mile which includes London Bridge and is distinguished by fine commercial and religious buildings; also—until just recently—by the Billingsgate fish market. It is much the same neighborhood as in T. S. Eliot's *The Waste Land*.

Only a few years earlier, William Blake had written (see p. 103) of the same London at midnight:

> I wander thro' each charter'd street,
> Near where the charter'd Thames does flow.
> And mark in every face I meet
> Marks of weakness, marks of woe.

Composed upon Westminster Bridge, September 3, 1802

Earth has not anything to show more fair:
Dull would he be of soul who could pass by
A sight so touching in its majesty:
This City now doth, like a garment, wear
The beauty of the morning; silent, bare,

Ships, towers, domes, theaters, and temples lie
Open unto the fields, and to the sky;
All bright and glittering in the smokeless air.
Never did sun more beautifully steep
In his first splendor, valley, rock, or hill;
Ne'er saw I, never felt, a calm so deep!
The river glideth at his own sweet will:
Dear God! the very houses seem asleep;
And all that mighty heart is lying still!

53

THE SPLENDOR FALLS

~

Alfred, Lord Tennyson

*T*he subtitle of Tennyson's *The Princess* is *A Medley*—and that is accurate and honest: there are a couple of narrative levels along with several songs that have achieved an independent celebrity. "Sweet and Low" and "Tears, Idle Tears" are known to readers who do not know *The Princess* and, conceivably, may not know Tennyson. "O Swallow, Swallow" returns at the end of T. S. Eliot's *The Waste Land.*

Having mentioned Eliot, we might as well go on to point out that his "Lines to a Duck in the Park" begins, "The long light shakes across the lake" and ends with an echo of Andrew Marvell's "To His Coy Mistress" (p. 27):

> For I know, and so should you
> That soon the enquiring worm shall try
> Our well-preserved complacency.

Of all the poets represented in these pages, Tennyson may be the most versatile: "Ulysses" (p. 201) is an ideal dramatic monologue; "The Eagle" (p. 204) is a perfect fragment; "Crossing the Bar" (p. 132) is everything a valediction ought to be. "The Splendor Falls" comes as close to the spirit of song and music as any words can come. Perhaps in compensation for weak eyesight, but probably for deeper, better reasons—such as genius—Tennyson had the finest "ear" of any nineteenth-century poet with the possible exception of Keats.

The Splendor Falls

The splendor falls on castle walls
    And snowy summits old in story;
The long light shakes across the lakes,
    And the wild cataract leaps in glory.
Blow, bugle, blow, set the wild echoes flying,
Blow, bugle; answer, echoes, dying, dying, dying.

O, hark, O, hear! how thin and clear,
   And thinner, clearer, farther going!
O, sweet and far from cliff and scar
   The horns of Elfland faintly blowing!
Blow, let us hear the purple glens replying,
Blow, bugle; answer, echoes, dying, dying, dying.

O love, they die in yon rich sky,
   They faint on hill or field or river;
Our echoes roll from soul to soul,
   And grow for ever and for ever.
Blow, bugle, blow, set the wild echoes flying,
And answer, echoes, answer, dying, dying, dying.

54

THE DARKLING THRUSH

~

Thomas Hardy

---

*A*ny number of poets have also been prose-writers, but Thomas Hardy enjoys two virtually unique distinctions: first, he wrote both poetry and prose with superlative genius; second, he wrote most of the prose *before* writing most of the poetry. Almost all other writers who do both do the poetry first. Hardy, in this as in other ways an individualist, had a thirty-year fiction-writing career, culminating in the twin masterpieces *Tess of the d'Urbervilles* and *Jude the Obscure,* and then went on to another thirty-year career in poetry, publishing his first book of verse in 1898, when he was already fifty-eight years old. Seven other volumes of verse were published between then and the year of his death, 1928.

"The Darkling Thrush" is dated "31st December 1900," to indicate that the poem is to be construed as set on the last day of the nineteenth century (actually, it was published in a magazine a few days before that date). The day is the last of the month, the year, and the century; the time is evening. (Think: "century" means "hundred," which means that the first century runs from 1 to 100, and the nineteenth century ran from 1801 through the end of 1900; soon we'll need to be educated into believing that 2000 is the last year of the twentieth century and not the first of the twenty-first). The poem is also poised on a threshold-gate, and there are two acts of *leaning* in the poem.

See also the introduction to Hopkins's "The Windhover" (p. 64).

The Darkling Thrush

I leant upon a coppice gate
    When Frost was specter-gray,
And Winter's dregs made desolate
    The weakening eye of day.
The tangled bine-stems scored the sky
    Like strings of broken lyres,
And all mankind that haunted nigh
    Had sought their household fires.

The land's sharp features seemed to be
    The Century's corpse outleant,
His crypt the cloudy canopy,
    The wind his death-lament.
The ancient pulse of germ and birth
    Was shrunken hard and dry,
And every spirit upon earth
    Seemed fervorless as I.

At once a voice arose among
    The bleak twigs overhead
In a full-hearted evensong
    Of joy illimited;
An aged thrush, frail, gaunt, and small,
    In blast-beruffled plume,
Had chosen thus to fling his soul
    Upon the growing gloom.

So little cause for carolings
    Of such ecstatic sound
Was written on terrestrial things
    Afar or nigh around,
That I could think there trembled through
    His happy good-night air
Some blessed Hope, whereof he knew
    And I was unaware.

55

LOVELIEST OF TREES, THE CHERRY NOW

~

A. E. Housman

A. E. Housman's first and best book was called *A Shropshire Lad,* but Housman was not from Shropshire and he was hardly a "lad" in 1895 when most of the poems were written. (It seems he went into a trancelike state of obsessive composition brought on by the shocking bad news from Oscar Wilde's terrible trials during that year.)

Shropshire man or not, lad or not, Housman used the persona called Terence Hearsay to express many of the Romantic sentiments of the late nineteenth century, almost as though in conscious continuation of the mood of Byron's "So, We'll Go No More a-Roving" (p. 141). Housman adds a tender stoicism not explicit in Byron.

Loveliest of Trees, the Cherry Now

Loveliest of trees, the cherry now
Is hung with bloom along the bough,
And stands about the woodland ride
Wearing white for Eastertide.

Now, of my threescore years and ten,
Twenty will not come again,
And take from seventy springs a score,
It only leaves me fifty more.

And since to look at things in bloom
Fifty springs are little room,
About the woodlands I will go
To see the cherry hung with snow.

56

MENDING WALL

~

Robert Frost

*T*he sentiment can be traced back to *Poor Richard's Almanac,* but the wording is Frost's own, so that he is alone among modern poets with the distinction of having composed a genuine proverb.

Few seem to have noticed how cynical that proverb is, and few likewise have bothered to distinguish Frost from his speaker or that speaker from the neighbor in the poem, who is, after all, a primitive, a hick, and a fool.

Some, eager to interpret even where interpretation is uncalled-for, have sought an Isolationist meaning in Frost's poem (which was published before World War I). Somewhat closer to home, one can read the poem as a justification for verse-form, which itself is a kind of fence or wall for containing the unruly fears and desires that motivate us.

Mending Wall

Something there is that doesn't love a wall,
That sends the frozen-ground-swell under it
And spills the upper boulders in the sun,
And makes gaps even two can pass abreast.
The work of hunters is another thing:
I have come after them and made repair
Where they have left not one stone on a stone,
But they would have the rabbit out of hiding,
To please the yelping dogs. The gaps I mean,
No one has seen them made or heard them made,
But at spring mending-time we find them there.
I let my neighbor know beyond the hill;
And on a day we meet to walk the line
And set the wall between us once again.
We keep the wall between us as we go.
To each the boulders that have fallen to each.
And some are loaves and some so nearly balls
We have to use a spell to make them balance:

"Stay where you are until our backs are turned!"
We wear our fingers rough with handling them.
Oh, just another kind of outdoor game,
One on a side. It comes to little more:
There where it is we do not need the wall:
He is all pine and I am apple orchard.
My apple trees will never get across
And eat the cones under his pines, I tell him.
He only says, "Good fences make good neighbors."
Spring is the mischief in me, and I wonder
If I could put a notion in his head:
"*Why* do they make good neighbors? Isn't it
Where there are cows? But here there are no cows.
Before I built a wall I'd ask to know
What I was walling in or walling out,
And to whom I was like to give offense.
Something there is that doesn't love a wall,
That wants it down." I could say "Elves" to him,
But it's not elves exactly, and I'd rather
He said it for himself. I see him there,
Bringing a stone grasped firmly by the top
In each hand, like an old-stone savage armed.
He moves in darkness as it seems to me,
Not of woods only and the shade of trees.
He will not go behind his father's saying,
And he likes having thought of it so well
He says again, "Good fences make good neighbors."

57

FERN HILL

~

Dylan Thomas

Thomas was said to be President Jimmy Carter's favorite poet, and at least one of Thomas's poems—the early "And Death Shall Have No Dominion"— has been quoted in episodes of two popular television series, "Beauty and the Beast" and "A Man Called Hawk." And Bob Dylan took his name from the great Welsh poet.

Thomas was in some ways a primitive and in some ways a thoroughgoing modernist, but in "Fern Hill" he produced a great ode in a complex stanza that could have been devised by Donne or Keats.

The name "Fern Hill" refers to Thomas's aunt's country house, where he spent some time as a boy, but its more general and more significant reference is to the fertility and shapeliness of organic and inorganic nature, of which humankind is both part and not a part.

Thomas had the good fortune to flourish just as the long-playing phonograph record came along, in the late 1940s and early 1950s. On top of his genius as a writer of poetry, he also had a prodigious gift for reading it; there are people who know little about poetry but who will never forget that grand voice intoning, "Now as I was young and easy under the apple boughs. . . ."

Fern Hill

Now as I was young and easy under the apple boughs
About the lilting house and happy as the grass was green,
    The night above the dingle starry,
       Time let me hail and climb
     Golden in the heydays of his eyes,
And honored among wagons I was prince of the apple towns
And once below a time I lordly had the trees and leaves
      Trail with daisies and barley
    Down the rivers of the windfall light.

And as I was green and carefree, famous among the barns
About the happy yard and singing as the farm was home,

In the sun that is young once only,
　　　Time let me play and be
　　Golden in the mercy of his means,
And green and golden I was huntsman and herdsman, the calves
Sang to my horn, the foxes on the hills barked clear and cold,
　　　And the sabbath rang slowly
　　In the pebbles of the holy streams.

All the sun long it was running, it was lovely, the hay
Fields high as the house, the tunes from the chimneys, it was air
　　　And playing, lovely and watery
　　　　And fire green as grass.
　　　And nightly under the simple stars
As I rode to sleep the owls were bearing the farm away,
All the moon long I heard, blessed among stables, the nightjars
　　　Flying with the ricks, and the horses
　　　　Flashing into the dark.

And then to awake, and the farm, like a wanderer white
With the dew, come back, the cock on his shoulder: it was all
　　　Shining, it was Adam and maiden,
　　　The sky gathered again
　　And the sun grew round that very day.
So it must have been after the birth of the simple light
In the first, spinning place, the spellbound horses walking warm
　　　Out of the whinnying green stable
　　　　On to the fields of praise.

And honored among foxes and pheasants by the gay house
Under the new made clouds and happy as the heart was long,
　　　In the sun born over and over,
　　　　I ran my heedless ways,
　　My wishes raced through the house high hay
And nothing I cared, at my sky blue trades, that time allows
In all his tuneful turning so few and such morning songs
　　　Before the children green and golden
　　　Follow him out of grace,

Nothing I cared, in the lamb white days, that time would take me
Up to the swallow thronged loft by the shadow of my hand,
　　In the moon that is always rising,

Nor that riding to sleep
I should hear him fly with the high fields
And wake to the farm forever fled from the childless land.
Oh as I was young and easy in the mercy of his means,
Time held me green and dying
Though I sang in my chains like the sea.

58

A LITANY IN TIME OF PLAGUE

~

Thomas Nashe

*N*ashe's comedy *Summer's Last Will and Testament* contains two songs that have outlasted their original setting: "Spring, the Sweet Spring" (with a bird-chorus that survives into Eliot's *The Waste Land:* "Cuckoo, jug-jug, pu-we, to-witta-woo!") and, in a much darker mood, this litany. (A formal church litany involves clergy and congregation alternating supplications and responses.)

Nashe could be trendy and forward-looking, as in his pioneering proto-novel *The Unfortunate Traveler; or, The Life of Jack Wilton;* this plague-time litany, however, looks back to the Middle Ages, a time that favored primitive simplicity and monotony and, seemingly, never got tired of hearing the same ideas (*topoi,* or commonplaces) supported by the same examples (*exempla*) and metaphors (*figurae*) over and over. This poem belongs in the category of The Vanity of Human Wishes; among its familiar examples are Helen and Hector, and a conspicuously conventional metaphor equates Earth and a stage.

The litany was not necessarily an idiom that required originality, and it has been argued that it takes no less genius to do a familiar thing in a refreshing way than to invent a new thing to do. Nashe's song is vividly clear in its images—

> Brightness falls from the air;
> Queens have died young and fair—

and touchingly confessional in certain details. We can hear Nashe, notoriously witty and wanton and bitter and artful, in the castigation of "vain art" and in the plangent couplet,

> Wit with his wantonness
> Tasteth death's bitterness.

A Litany in Time of Plague

Adieu, farewell, earth's bliss;
This world uncertain is;
Fond are life's lustful joys;
Death proves of them all but toys;

None from his darts can fly;
I am sick, I must die.
    Lord, have mercy on us!

Rich men, trust not in wealth,
Gold cannot buy you health;
Physic himself must fade.
All things to end are made,
The plague full swift goes by;
I am sick, I must die
    Lord, have mercy on us!

Beauty is but a flower
Which wrinkles will devour;
Brightness falls from the air;
Queens have died young and fair;
Dust hath closed Helen's eye.
I am sick, I must die.
    Lord, have mercy on us!

Strength stoops unto the grave,
Worms feed on Hector brave;
Swords may not fight with fate,
Earth still holds ope her gate.
"Come, come" the bells do cry.
I am sick, I must die.
    Lord, have mercy on us.

Wit with his wantonness
Tasteth death's bitterness;
Hell's executioner
Hath no ears for to hear
What vain art can reply.
I am sick, I must die.
    Lord, have mercy on us.

Haste, therefore, each degree,
To welcome destiny;
Heaven is our heritage,
Earth but a player's stage;
Mount we unto the sky.
I am sick, I must die.
    Lord, have mercy on us.

59

SONG: TO CELIA

~

Ben Jonson

It is unlikely that many among the general reading public will know poems
in this collection as true *lyrics,* that is to say, as songs to be sung. But this gem
of Jonson's is still, after almost four hundred years, one of the loveliest and
most popular of songs in English.

Song: To Celia

Drink to me only with thine eyes,
    And I will pledge with mine;
Or leave a kiss but in the cup,
    And I'll not look for wine.
The thirst that from the soul doth rise
    Doth ask a drink divine;
But might I of Jove's nectar sup,
    I would not change for thine.
I sent thee late a rosy wreath,
    Not so much honoring thee
As giving it a hope that there
    It could not withered be.
But thou thereon didst only breathe,
    And sent'st it back to me;
Since when it grows, and smells, I swear,
    Not of itself, but thee.

60

THE COLLAR

~

George Herbert

The God in Herbert's poems may seem peculiarly personal and therefore more Protestant than Catholic. Herbert's volume of poetry is called *The Temple,* but the emphasis in the poems is on one's direct relationship with God. We may also detect here some echoes of the Psalms of David, many of which address or praise a personal God.

We may suspect that Herbert loads the dice or stacks the deck for thirty-two lines, making a very persuasive case for escaping the "rope of sands" of the religious life; but, really, the thirty-two-line argument seems strong and sincere; otherwise Herbert *would* be cheating.

The "board" that is struck in the first line is a table—a usage that survives today only in such locations as "bed and board."

The Collar

I struck the board, and cried, No more.
        I will abroad.
    What? shall I ever sigh and pine?
My lines and life are free; free as the road,
    Loose as the wind, as large as store.
       Shall I be still in suit?
    Have I no harvest but a thorn
    To let me blood, and not restore
What I have lost with cordial fruit?
       Sure there was wine
Before my sighs did dry it: there was corn
    Before my tears did drown it.
    Is the year only lost to me?
      Have I no bays to crown it?
No flowers, no garlands gay? all blasted?
       All wasted?
Not so, my heart: but there is fruit,
      And thou hast hands.
Recover all thy sigh-blown age

On double pleasures: leave thy cold dispute
Of what is fit, and not. Forsake thy cage,
        Thy rope of sands,
Which petty thoughts have made, and made to thee
    Good cable, to enforce and draw,
        And be thy law,
   While thou didst wink and wouldst not see.
       Away, Take Heed,
       I will abroad,
Call in thy death's head there: tie up thy fears.
       He that forbears
     To suit and serve his need,
      Deserves his load.
But as I raved and grew more fierce and wild
      At every word,
Me thought I heard one calling, *Child!*
     And I replied, *My Lord.*

61

WHY SO PALE AND WAN, FOND LOVER?

~

Sir John Suckling

Some authorities give Suckling credit for inventing the game of cribbage, which has furnished thousands of people with thousands of hours of entertainment. Surely that kind of thing is some degree of treasure in heaven.

Card games and songs both call for orderly arrangement of simple parts with complex engagements among contestants. "Why So Pale and Wan, Fond Lover?" is an easy song, to be sure, but it has a good deal of prosodic sophistication as well as rhetorical drama: in one dimension, the speaker works against the lover (who may be himself); in another, the speaker and lover together work against the woman. And the percussively reiterated questions work against the final imperative, "Quit, quit."

Why So Pale and Wan, Fond Lover?

Why so pale and wan, fond lover?
    Prithee, why so pale?
Will, when looking well can't move her,
    Looking ill prevail?
    Prithee, why so pale?

Why so dull and mute, young sinner?
    Prithee, why so mute?
Will, when speaking well can't win her,
    Saying nothing do 't?
    Prithee, why so mute?

Quit, quit, for shame; this will not move,
    This cannot take her.
If of herself she will not love,
    Nothing can make her:
    The devil take her!

62

THE GARDEN

~

Andrew Marvell

*T*his poem sounds almost like a post-Rachel-Carson plea for the protection of the natural environment—and also like a realistic denial of symbolism.

Marvell ridicules the use of certain trees for emblematic purposes (palms for jocks, oaks for politicians, bays for poetry) and highlights the genuine cruelty of carving names in the bark of trees. Marvell, furthermore, offers a radically revisionist reading of classical and scriptural myths, suggesting that the metamorphoses of Daphne and Syrinx into laurel and reed were by design; and that Adam's loss of paradise dated from the introduction of Eve:

> Two paradises 'twere in one,
> To live in paradise alone.

These farfetched conceits place Marvell among the seventeenth-century Metaphysicals, who specialized in such shocking conduct. Even after three centuries, there is still a measure of surprise in the lines

> Annihilating all that's made
> To a green thought in a green shade—

thanks to the contrast between the Latinate absoluteness of the first of these lines and the Germanic reality of the second. The juxtaposition of the conventional "green shade" and the surrealist "green thought" also remains surprising and delightful.

The Garden

How vainly men themselves amaze
To win the palm, the oak, or bays,
And their incessant labors see
Crown'd from some single herb or tree,
Whose short and narrow-vergèd shade
Does prudently their toils upbraid;
While all the flowers and trees do close
To weave the garlands of repose!

Fair Quiet, have I found thee here,
And Innocence thy sister dear?
Mistaken long, I sought you then
In busy companies of men:
Your sacred plants, if here below,
Only among the plants will grow:
Society is all but rude
To this delicious solitude.

No white nor red was ever seen
So amorous as this lovely green.
Fond lovers, cruel as their flame,
Cut in these trees their mistress' name:
Little, alas! they know or heed
How far these beauties hers exceed!
Fair trees! wheres'e'er your barks I wound,
No name shall but your own be found.

When we have run our passions' heat,
Love hither makes his best retreat:
The gods, that mortal beauty chase,
Still in a tree did end their race;
Apollo hunted Daphne so
Only that she might laurel grow;
And Pan did after Syrinx speed
Not as a nymph, but for a reed.

What wondrous life is this I lead!
Ripe apples drop about my head;
The luscious clusters of the vine
Upon my mouth do crush their wine;
The nectarine and curious peach
Into my hands themselves do reach;
Stumbling on melons, as I pass,
Ensnared with flowers, I fall on grass.

Meanwhile the mind from pleasure less
Withdraws into its happiness;
The mind, that ocean where each kind
Does straight its own resemblance find;
Yet it creates, transcending these,

Far other worlds, and other seas;
Annihilating all that's made
To a green thought in a green shade.

Here at the fountain's sliding foot,
Or at some fruit-tree's mossy root,
Casting the body's vest aside,
My soul into the boughs does glide;
There, like a bird, it sits and sings,
Then whets and combs its silver wings,
And, till prepared for longer flight,
Waves in its plumes the various light.

Such was that happy Garden-state
While man there walk'd without a mate:
After a place so pure and sweet,
What other help could yet be meet!
But 'twas beyond a mortal's share
To wander solitary there:
Two paradises 'twere in one,
To live in Paradise alone.

How well the skilful gard'ner drew
Of flowers and herbs this dial new!
Where, from above, the milder sun
Does through a fragrant zodiac run:
And, as it works, th' industrious bee
Computes its time as well as we.
How could such sweet and wholesome hours
Be reckon'd, but with herbs and flowers!

63

THE SOLITARY REAPER

~

William Wordsworth

*A*lthough he derived most of his material from his own experience, Wordsworth acknowledged that this vision of a lone working-woman singing in the Erse language came to him from a book: Thomas Wilkinson's *Tour of Scotland*. The poet asks, "Will no one tell me what she sings?" because he cannot understand her language.

The Solitary Reaper

Behold her, single in the field,
Yon solitary Highland Lass!
Reaping and singing by herself;
Stop here, or gently pass!
Alone she cuts and binds the grain,
And sings a melancholy strain;
O listen! for the Vale profound
Is overflowing with the sound.

No Nightingale did ever chaunt
More welcome notes to weary bands
Of travelers in some shady haunt,
Among Arabian sands:
A voice so thrilling ne'er was heard
In spring-time from the Cuckoo-bird,
Breaking the silence of the seas
Among the farthest Hebrides.

Will no one tell me what she sings? —
Perhaps the plaintive numbers flow
For old, unhappy, far-off things,
And battles long ago:
Or is it some more humble lay,
Familiar matter of today?
Some natural sorrow, loss, or pain,
That has been, and may be again?

Whate'er the theme, the Maiden sang
As if her song could have no ending;
I saw her singing at her work,
And o'er the sickle bending:—
I listened, motionless and still;
And, as I mounted up the hill,
The music in my heart I bore,
Long after it was heard no more.

64

BREAK, BREAK, BREAK

~

Alfred, Lord Tennyson

---

*L*ord Byron, who was one of Tennyson's earliest exemplars, had addressed the ocean memorably in *Childe Harold's Pilgrimage:*

> Roll on, thou deep and dark blue Ocean—roll!

And we accept the appropriateness of the gesture, although it may seem fruitless to tell an inanimate object to keep on doing what it can't help doing anyway.

Symbolic or symbol-provoking oceans and seas haunt the poetry of the past two centuries—from Wordsworth and Byron through Tennyson and Arnold, on to Stevens, Frost, Eliot, Lowell, and Ammons. On a smaller scale, Tennyson employed "The Brook" for a similar contrast ("For men may come and men may go,/ But I go on forever").

It is probable that "Break, Break, Break" refers to the death of Tennyson's friend Arthur Henry Hallam, who is also the subject of the great elegy *In Memoriam.*

Break, Break, Break

Break, break, break,
    On thy cold gray stones, O Sea!
And I would that my tongue could utter
    The thoughts that arise in me.

O, well for the fisherman's boy,
    That he shouts with his sister at play!
O, well for the sailor lad,
    That he sings in his boat on the bay!

And the stately ships go on
    To their haven under the hill;
But O for the touch of a vanished hand,
    And the sound of a voice that is still!

Break, break, break,
　　At the foot of thy crags, O Sea!
But the tender grace of a day that is dead
　　Will never come back to me.

65

CROSSING THE BAR

~

Alfred, Lord Tennyson

*T*ennyson wrote "Crossing the Bar" when he was eighty and, although he went on to write other poems, he asked that this one be placed at the end of all collections of his poetry. Tennyson showed a fine sense of fitness in writing the poem in the first place, with its noble religious stoicism and good Britannic sea imagery, and also in dictating its placement.

The "bar" would be a sandbar exposed and uncrossable at low tide but covered at high tide.

Crossing the Bar

Sunset and evening star,
 And one clear call for me!
And may there be no moaning of the bar,
 When I put out to sea,

But such a tide as moving seems asleep,
 Too full for sound and foam,
When that which drew from out the boundless deep
 Turns again home.

Twilight and evening bell,
 And after that the dark!
And may there be no sadness of farewell,
 When I embark;

For though from out our bourne of Time and Place
 The flood may bear me far,
I hope to see my Pilot face to face
 When I have crossed the bar.

66

MR. FLOOD'S PARTY
~
Edwin Arlington Robinson

*L*ike Robinson's "Miniver Cheevy" (p. 144), "Mr. Flood's Party" is an episode in the wretched history of Tilbury Town, where the "village virus" drives some good people to drink.

Both the "Mr." and the "Party" of the title are ironic, since Eben Flood is alone. The viewpoint is somewhat detached and disinterested, but the poet contributes some tender touches here and there. By simply asserting the presence of "two moons" (instead of belaboring the point that drunkenness caused Flood to see double), the poem enters into the character's consciousness. The comparisons to a mother and the heroic knight Roland (recounted in the kind of medieval poem that Miniver Cheevy and maybe Mr. Flood too would have liked) also add sympathy to the sketch of Mr. Flood. His besotted state is hardly defended or justified, but neither is it condemned as a moral flaw too awful to forgive.

Mr. Flood's Party

Old Eben Flood, climbing alone one night
Over the hill between the town below
And the forsaken upland hermitage
That held as much as he should ever know
On earth again of home, paused warily.
The road was his with not a native near;
And Eben, having leisure, said aloud,
For no man else in Tilbury Town to hear:

"Well, Mr. Flood, we have the harvest moon
Again, and we may not have many more;
The bird is on the wing, the poet says,
And you and I have said it here before.
Drink to the bird." He raised up to the light
The jug that he had gone so far to fill,
And answered huskily: "Well, Mr. Flood,
Since you propose it, I believe I will."

Alone, as if enduring to the end
A valiant armor of scarred hopes outworn,
He stood there in the middle of the road
Like Roland's ghost winding a silent horn.
Below him, in the town among the trees,
Where friends of other days had honored him,
A phantom salutation of the dead
Rang thinly till old Eben's eyes were dim.

Then, as a mother lays her sleeping child
Down tenderly, fearing it may awake,
He set the jug down slowly at his feet
With trembling care, knowing that most things break;
And only when assured that on firm earth
It stood, as the uncertain lives of men
Assuredly did not, he paced away,
And with his hand extended paused again:

"Well, Mr. Flood, we have not met like this
In a long time; and many a change has come
To both of us, I fear, since last it was
We had a drop together. Welcome home!"
Convivially returning with himself,
Again he raised the jug up to the light;
And with an acquiescent quaver said:
"Well, Mr. Flood, if you insist, I might.

"Only a very little, Mr. Flood—
For auld lang syne. No more, sir; that will do."
So, for the time, apparently it did,
And Eben evidently thought so too;
For soon amid the silver loneliness
Of night he lifted up his voice and sang,
Secure, with only two moons listening,
Until the whole harmonious landscape rang—

"For auld lang syne." The weary throat gave out,
The last word wavered; and the song being done,
He raised again the jug regretfully
And shook his head, and was again alone.
There was not much that was ahead of him,
And there was nothing in the town below—
Where strangers would have shut the many doors
That many friends had opened long ago.

67

MUSÉE DES BEAUX ARTS

~

W. H. Auden

When he put together his 1945 volume of *Collected Poems,* Auden arranged the contents of the main body, not by chronology or subject, but in alphabetical order according to the first word. This poem, beginning "About," happened to come first by that whimsically arbitrary practice, which gave this one a prominence that it scarcely deserves, since Auden probably wrote at least a dozen better poems.

As a didactic work that discusses art history, the poem fails: the first sentence is unjustifiably contorted (it would be better as "The Old Masters were never wrong about suffering"); besides, the sentiment is all wet, since the Old Masters did not agree about anything under the sun, and few of them treat suffering as eccentrically as Brueghel did in *Landscape with the Fall of Icarus* (also, by the way, the subject of a poem by William Carlos Williams).

As a mimetic work, however, that does not discuss anything but rather presents a character, the poem succeeds very well indeed. Someone with suffering on his or her mind—probably because of a painful personal experience—seeks consolation in a foreign art museum, probably in Brussels, where many Brueghels are housed. After an off-center beginning—"About suffering they were never wrong"—the speaker discovers a highly conditional truth about suffering (including one's own) and arrives at a point of stoical equilibrium and something like calm.

Musée des Beaux Arts

About suffering they were never wrong,
The Old Masters: how well they understood
Its human position; how it takes place
While someone else is eating or opening a window or just walking
    dully along;
How, when the aged are reverently, passionately waiting
For the miraculous birth, there always must be
Children who did not specially want it to happen, skating

On a pond at the edge of the wood:
They never forgot
That even the dreadful martyrdom must run its course
Anyhow in a corner, some untidy spot
Where the dogs go on with their doggy life and the torturer's horse
Scratches its innocent behind on a tree.

In Brueghel's *Icarus,* for instance: how everything turns away
Quite leisurely from the disaster; the plowman may
Have heard the splash, the forsaken cry,
But for him it was not an important failure; the sun shone
As it had to on the white legs disappearing into the green
Water; and the expensive delicate ship that must have seen
Something amazing, a boy falling out of the sky,
Had somewhere to get to and sailed calmly on.

68

THE DEATH OF THE BALL TURRET GUNNER

~

Randall Jarrell

Only three or four of the poems herein have to do with the war dead, and the modern ones (by Owen and Jarrell) have to do with the humble and youthful casualties reduced to anonymity and ashes by our worst crime.

Jarrell served in the Army Air Corps (later the Air Force) during World War II, and, although not himself a pilot, was familiar with the design of bombers like the B-17 and B-24 that had a plexiglass turret mounted on their undersides for protection against fighters attacking from below. As Jarrell noted, these fighters were "armed with cannon firing explosive shells." (He added, "The hose was a steam hose.")

Karl Shapiro said Jarrell wrote "the most famous and the best war poem of anyone in the twentieth century, in five lines."

The Death of the Ball Turret Gunner

From my mother's sleep I fell into the State
And I hunched in its belly till my wet fur froze.
Six miles from earth, loosed from its dream of life,
I woke to black flak and the nightmare fighters.
When I died they washed me out of the turret with a hose.

69

FULL FATHOM FIVE

~

William Shakespeare

In *The Tempest,* the spirit Ariel sings this little song to Ferdinand, who believes that his father, the King of Naples, has been drowned in a shipwreck. Ferdinand is wrong, as Ariel knows, so that the potential cruelty in the message is softened somewhat.

Ferdinand may in fact be comforted in that the horror of death by water is mitigated by the transformation of the body into precious lovely substances like coral and pearl.

Full Fathom Five

Full fathom five thy father lies;
    Of his bones are coral made;
Those are pearls that were his eyes:
    Nothing of him that doth fade
But doth suffer a sea-change
Into something rich and strange.
Sea-nymphs hourly ring his knell:
    Ding-dong.
Hark! now I hear them,—ding-dong, bell.

70

WHEN TO THE SESSIONS OF SWEET SILENT THOUGHT

~

William Shakespeare

*H*ere we see an exoskeleton as distinct as a grasshopper's: "When . . . Then . . . Then . . . But . . . ." And the vocabulary owes much to law and commerce. The "sessions" and "summon" both refer to law. "Expense" means "loss," and "account" has its usual literary sense far from what accountants and bank-tellers do, but the "pay" is still the language of money.

This sonnet belongs to a category called "complaint," a favorite with English poets from Chaucer to the present. Here, as in celebrated soliloquies in *Macbeth* and *Hamlet,* Shakespeare seems to relish the chance to make an inventory of woes. But the "But" at the end brings in a new note of felicity that, I must say, seems rather perfunctory and mechanical. This is the formulaic gimmick that made Gertrude Stein complain that, whereas Shakespeare's plays were written as they were written (that is, organically), the sonnets were written as they were going to be written (that is, according to a predetermined recipe). Even so, many sensitive readers find the poem very moving.

When to the Sessions of Sweet Silent Thought

When to the sessions of sweet silent thought
I summon up remembrance of things past,
I sigh the lack of many a thing I sought,
And with old woes new wail my dear time's waste.
Then can I drown an eye, unus'd to flow,
For precious friends hid in death's dateless night,
And weep afresh love's long since cancell'd woe,
And moan th' expense of many a vanish'd sight.
Then can I grieve at grievances foregone,
And heavily from woe to woe tell o'er
The sad account of fore-bemoaned moan,
Which I new pay as if not paid before.
    But if the while I think on thee, dear friend,
    All losses are restor'd and sorrows end.

71

PIPING DOWN THE VALLEYS WILD

~

William Blake

*B*lake introduces his *Songs of Innocence* with a song of innocence *of sorts* — it is innocence without idiocy, innocence with sophistication. There is some weeping along with the laughter (as is true of babies and adults alike), and there must be some misgiving in the recognition that the passage from piping and singing to writing is a downward motion that involves a stain on clarity.

Piping down the Valleys Wild

Piping down the valleys wild
Piping songs of pleasant glee
On a cloud I saw a child,
And he laughing said to me,

"Pipe a song about a Lamb";
So I piped with merry chear.
"Piper pipe that song again" —
So I piped, he wept to hear.

"Drop thy pipe thy happy pipe
Sing thy songs of happy chear";
So I sung the same again
While he wept with joy to hear.

"Piper sit thee down and write
In a book that all may read" —
So he vanish'd from my sight.
And I pluck'd a hollow reed,

And I made a rural pen,
And I stain'd the water clear,
And I wrote my happy songs
Every child may joy to hear.

72

SO, WE'LL GO NO MORE A-ROVING

~

George Gordon Noel Byron, 6th Baron Byron

*B*yron was partly Scottish, and in his earlier poetry he followed the lead of such other Scots as Robert Burns and Sir Walter Scott in reviving old ballads and composing new ones—or, as here, of grafting new material onto old.

A song of regretful decrepitude may seem fatuous for a writer who was not yet thirty; indeed, Byron's power and eloquence in expressing just such mournful feelings account for his enduring popularity with young readers, even though they may know as well as we (and Byron) that the attitude is largely bogus. But we know that Byron was quite sincere and that he had scarcely seven more years to live when he wrote the song. We ought to remember that what actuaries call "life expectancy" was much shorter two hundred years ago.

So, We'll Go No More a-Roving

So, we'll go no more a-roving
  So late into the night,
Though the heart be still as loving,
  And the moon be still as bright.

For the sword outwears its sheath,
  And the soul wears out the breast,
And the heart must pause to breathe,
  And love itself have rest.

Though the night was made for loving,
  And the day returns too soon,
Yet we'll go no more a-roving
  By the light of the moon.

73

I HEARD A FLY BUZZ

~

Emily Dickinson

*A*lthough I have not made a scrupulous study of such things, I have the feeling that poems written, as it were, from beyond the grave are largely by Americans (I'm thinking of Dickinson's "Because I Could Not Stop for Death," p. 62, and Jarrell's "The Death of the Ball Turret Gunner," p. 137, along with some poems by Poe that are not in this collection).

Dickinson lived at a time when conditions (health, sanitation, medicine, nutrition) favored large families, but illness and death were all around, especially the death of the young, including infants. It is probable that Dickinson, born in 1830, had more firsthand experience of death than most people born in 1930. In any event, she witnessed much suffering and death, and wrote about it profoundly and abundantly. (The false or comic side of the coin is represented by Julia A. Moore, the "Sweet Singer of Michigan," and Bloodgood Havilland Cutter, the "Farmer Poet of Long Island," both of whom were ridiculed by Mark Twain in *Huckleberry Finn, The Innocents Abroad,* and elsewhere.)

Dickinson's fly in some ways has more tangible, terrifying reality than Melville's whale or Poe's raven. It is a fly, first and foremost, a very fly. It is rendered in its full fly-hood of things heard and seen, as well as with "Blue— uncertain stumbling Buzz"—when, of course, it is a symbol, a veritable transcendental emblem. Yes, yes, but it is still a *fly.*

I Heard a Fly Buzz

I heard a Fly buzz—when I died—
The Stillness in the Room
Was like the Stillness in the Air—
Between the Heaves of Storm—

The Eyes around—had wrung them dry—
And Breaths were gathering firm
For that last Onset—when the King
Be witnessed—in the Room—

I willed my Keepsakes—Signed away
What portion of me be
Assignable—and then it was
There interposed a Fly—

With Blue—uncertain stumbling Buzz—
Between the light—and me—
And then the Windows failed—and then
I could not see to see—

74

MINIVER CHEEVY

~

Edwin Arlington Robinson

---

*R*obinson was like many other modern writers—Thomas Hardy, Arnold Bennett, Sherwood Anderson, Edgar Lee Masters, Sinclair Lewis, William Faulkner—in his capacity for creating not only a gallery of representative characters but also a town or region for them to live and die in. Robinson's "Tilbury Town," which is associated with his boyhood in Maine, resembles Anderson's "Winesburg" and Masters's "Spoon River"—little places afflicted with what has been called the "village virus," a disease of a community too urbanized to offer the rewards of country living but too small to offer the rewards of city life. The virus-stricken citizens are good and promising people who are disappointed and demoralized by their environments, which stimulate desires and ambitions but offer no authentic ways of fulfilling them. Nowadays, when the towns and villages have given way to suburbs, it may be that nothing essential has changed, and the hardy virus persists in some new and improved strains.

"Miniver Cheevy" is partly a lucid, ironic caricature of a common village type ridiculously in love with a Middle Ages that never existed, except in the imaginations of dozens of Romantic and Victorian writers; but it is partly a self-portrait as well: Robinson himself certainly "kept on drinking" (a common cause-and-effect of the village virus), and in his later years he wrote some notoriously inert poems on Arthurian subjects. But at the time of writing "Miniver Cheevy" (around 1910) Robinson was wide-awake and thoroughly modern; for about one fifth of this century he was, deservedly, the most popular of the serious American poets.

Miniver Cheevy

Miniver Cheevy, child of scorn,
    Grew lean while he assailed the seasons;
He wept that he was ever born,
    And he had reasons.

Miniver loved the days of old
  When swords were bright and steeds were prancing;
The vision of a warrior bold
  Would set him dancing.

Miniver sighed for what was not,
  And dreamed, and rested from his labors;
He dreamed of Thebes and Camelot,
  And Priam's neighbors.

Miniver mourned the ripe renown
  That made so many a name so fragrant;
He mourned Romance, now on the town,
  And Art, a vagrant.

Miniver loved the Medici,
  Albeit he had never seen one;
He would have sinned incessantly
  Could he have been one.

Miniver cursed the commonplace
  And eyed a khaki suit with loathing;
He missed the medieval grace
  Of iron clothing.

Miniver scorned the gold he sought,
  But sore annoyed was he without it;
Miniver thought, and thought, and thought,
  And thought about it.

Miniver Cheevy, born too late,
  Scratched his head and kept on thinking;
Miniver coughed, and called it fate,
  And kept on drinking.

75

TO BROOKLYN BRIDGE

~

Hart Crane

So powerful was T. S. Eliot's *The Waste Land* (1922) as an expression of collapse and failure that any number of writers hastened to respond in one form or another; Robert Frost's *New Hampshire* and William Carlos Williams's *Spring and All,* both of 1923, can be read as answers to *The Waste Land,* but no reply has been stronger than Hart Crane's prodigiously eloquent *The Bridge* (1930), which countered the Waste Land myth with its own myth: the Bridge.

Although Eliot was, like Crane, an American midwesterner, *The Waste Land* contains almost nothing of American history or literature. Crane's reaction was to write a poem that bridged the space between America and Europe and even the gap between engineering and aesthetics. No modern invention can match a suspension bridge for the combination of superlative usefulness and superlative beauty.

Crane's poem (of which this selection is the proem to the entire work) is a bridge in time, too: it reaches back to the pentameter quatrains of Thomas Gray's "Elegy Written in a Country Churchyard" (p. 40), with which it shares a final word, and forward to one of Philip Larkin's last poems, "A Bridge for the Living," which is also in pentameter quatrains and also likens a bridge to a harp.

Some critics have ridiculed Crane's effort to mix a modern scene of acetylene and traffic lights with an antiquated idiom of "thou dost" and so forth, but the consensus now is that Crane's only failure was in not quite achieving his own impossible ambition in his own terrific terms. It is to his everlasting credit that he had that ambition in the first place.

To Brooklyn Bridge

How many dawns, chill from his rippling rest
The seagull's wings shall dip and pivot him,
Shedding white rings of tumult, building high
Over the chained bay waters Liberty—

Then, with inviolate curve, forsake our eyes
As apparitional as sails that cross
Some page of figures to be filed away;
—Till elevators drop us from our day . . .

I think of cinemas, panoramic sleights
With multitudes bent toward some flashing scene
Never disclosed, but hastened to again,
Foretold to other eyes on the same screen;

And Thee, across the harbor, silver-paced
As though the sun took step of thee, yet left
Some motion ever unspent in thy stride,—
Implicitly thy freedom staying thee!

Out of some subway scuttle, cell or loft
A bedlamite speeds to thy parapets,
Tilting there momently, shrill shirt ballooning,
A jest falls from the speechless caravan.

Down Wall, from girder into street noon leaks,
A rip-tooth of the sky's acetylene;
All afternoon the cloud-flown derricks turn . . .
Thy cables breathe the North Atlantic still.

And obscure as that heaven of the Jews,
Thy guerdon . . . Accolade thou dost bestow
Of anonymity time cannot raise:
Vibrant reprieve and pardon thou dost show.

O harp and altar, of the fury fused,
(How could mere toil align thy choiring strings!)
Terrific threshold of the prophet's pledge,
Prayer of pariah, and the lover's cry,—

Again the traffic lights that skim thy swift
Unfractioned idiom, immaculate sigh of stars,
Beading thy path—condense eternity:
And we have seen night lifted in thine arms.

Under thy shadow by the piers I waited;
Only in darkness is thy shadow clear.
The City's fiery parcels all undone,
Already snow submerges an iron year . . .

O Sleepless as the river under thee,
Vaulting the sea, the prairies' dreaming sod,
Unto us lowliest sometime sweep, descend
And of the curveship lend a myth to God.

76

EDWARD, EDWARD

~

Anonymous

My remarks above on "Sir Patrick Spens" (p. 7) call it the more primitive of the two anonymous ballads in this book. Its design is a compressed narration of events with four focal speeches and a kind of moralizing epilogue.

"Edward, Edward" presents a quantum advance in sophistication and polish: the stanza is more complex, and the design is stripped to a set of quick *ex post facto* exchanges between a mother and a son. From the very outset, it is clear that the mother is crooked, for she obviously knows exactly why the sword is dripping with blood; Edward's answer is feebleness itself, since he had no earthly reason to kill either his hawk or his steed. Then, once he confesses what she must know already, she spends more than half of her half of the poem asking questions that deviously lead up to what is really on her mind: "And what will you leave to your own mother dear?"

As a matter of fact, neither this poem nor "Sir Patrick Spens" deserves to be called "primitive" in any sense; both satisfy modern demands for the dramatic and the imagistic. Neither goes much into motives: we never know why the "eldern knight" suggests Sir Patrick Spens for the fatal mission, nor do we know why the mother here got her son to murder his father. But we know that people do such things all the time. Since "Edward, Edward" concerns a strictly domestic drama, while "Sir Patrick Spens" touches on affairs of state, the former may seem a more touching (and shocking) work.

Edward, Edward

"Why does your brand so drop with blood,
    Edward, Edward?
Why does your brand so drop with blood,
  And why so sad go ye, O?"
"O I have killed my hawk so good,
    Mother, mother;
O I have killed my hawk so good,
  And I have no more but he, O."

"Your hawk's blood was never so red,
Edward, Edward;
Your hawk's blood was never so red,
My dear son, I tell thee, O."
"O I have killed my red-roan steed,
Mother, mother;
O I have killed my red-roan steed,
That went so fair and free, O."

"Your steed was old, and ye have more,
Edward, Edward;
Your steed was old, and you have more,
Some other dole ye dree, O."
"O I have killed my father dear,
Mother, mother;
O I have killed my father dear,
Alas, and woe is me, O!"

"And what penance will ye dree for that,
Edward, Edward?
What penance will ye dree for that,
My dear son, now tell me, O."
"I'll set my foot in yonder boat,
Mother, mother,
I'll set my foot in yonder boat,
And I'll fare o'er the sea, O."

"And what will ye do with your towers and your hall,
Edward, Edward?
And what will ye do with your towers and your hall,
That were so fair to see, O?"
"I'll let them stand till down they fall,
Mother, mother;
I'll let them stand till down they fall,
For here never more must I be, O."

"And what will ye leave to your bairns and your wife,
Edward, Edward?
And what will ye leave to your bairns and your wife,
When ye go o'er the sea, O?"

"The world's room: let them beg through life,
             Mother, mother;
The world's room: let them beg through life,
  For them never more will I see, O."

"And what will you leave to your own mother dear,
             Edward, Edward?
And what will ye leave to your own mother dear,
  My dear son, now tell me, O?"
"The curse of hell from me shall ye bear,
             Mother, mother;
The curse of hell from me shall ye bear,
  Such counsels ye gave to me, O!"

77

SINCE THERE'S NO HELP, COME LET US KISS AND PART

~

Michael Drayton

*D*rayton's *Idea* or *Ideas Mirrour* was published in 1594. It is thought that the lady called "Idea" is actually Anne Goodere, daughter of Drayton's patron.

Drayton was a year older than Shakespeare and, like Shakespeare, wrote a sequence of English sonnets during the 1590s, when the fad was at its height. But Drayton's language is much plainer than Shakespeare's; the introductory sonnet of *Idea* sounds quite modern: "My verse is the true image of my mind."

The first three lines of Sonnet LXI quoted here consist exclusively of ordinary monosyllables, and we might almost believe that this speaker is as serious and as free of irony as the Chaucer who could begin a rondel,

> Sin I fro Love escaped am so fat,
> I nevere thenke to been in his prison lene:
> Sin I am free, I counte him nat a bene.

But not quite.

Since There's No Help, Come Let Us Kiss and Part

Since there's no help, come let us kiss and part;
Nay, I have done, you get no more of me,
And I am glad, yea, glad with all my heart
That thus so cleanly I myself can free;
Shake hands for ever, cancel all our vows,
And when we meet at any time again,
Be it not seen in either of our brows
That we one jot of former love retain.
Now at the last gasp of Love's latest breath,
When, his pulse failing, Passion speechless lies,
When Faith is kneeling by his bed of death,
And Innocence is closing up his eyes,
Now if thou wouldst, when all have given him over,
From death to life thou mightst him yet recover.

78

OH MISTRESS MINE

~

William Shakespeare

Shakespeare's comedy *Twelfth Night* opens with the Duke's speech,

> If music be the food of love, play on,
> Give me excess of it, that, surfeiting,
> The appetite may sicken, and so die.

Harmonizing with that sentiment, accordingly, there are several songs in the play, including, in addition to this one, "Come Away, Come Away, Death" and "When That I Was and a Little Tiny Boy."

"Oh Mistress Mine," sung by the clown Feste, is as light as sea-foam. It oscillates cheerfully between nonsense and platitude, finally sounding the familiar refrain of *carpe diem* — "seize the day" — as in many Renaissance lyrics (for instance, "To the Virgins, to Make Much of Time," p. 26, and "To His Coy Mistress," p. 27).

Oh Mistress Mine

Oh mistress mine! where are you roaming?
Oh! stay and hear; your true love's coming,
   That can sing both high and low.
Trip no further, pretty sweeting;
Journeys end in lovers meeting,
   Every wise man's son doth know.

What is love? 'tis not hereafter;
Present mirth hath present laughter;
   What's to come is still unsure:
In delay there lies no plenty;
Then come kiss me, sweet and twenty,
   Youth's a stuff will not endure.

79

ON MY FIRST SON

~

Ben Jonson

*J*onson was a classical scholar, and his poem on the death of his first son, who died on his seventh birthday ("on the just day") in 1603, displays learning as well as a species of classical stoicism uncommon in English verse.

The boy was a junior, and, as Jonson knew, the name "Benjamin" means "son of the right hand," or "favorite." Jonson also knew that "poetry" means "things made" or "products," so that, by a reversible conceit, one may speak of one's poems as children and of one's children as poems.

On My First Son

Farewell, thou child of my right hand, and joy;
  My sin was too much hope of thee, loved boy.
Seven years thou wert lent to me, and I thee pay,
  Exacted by thy fate, on the just day.
Oh, could I lose all father now! For why
  Will man lament the state he should envy?
To have so soon 'scaped world's and flesh's rage,
  And, if no other misery, yet age?
Rest in soft peace, and, asked, say here doth lie
  Ben Jonson his best piece of poetry;
For whose sake, henceforth, all his vows be such,
  As what he loves may never like too much.

80

AT THE ROUND EARTH'S IMAGINED CORNERS

~

John Donne

*T*hree of Donne's "Holy Sonnets" are included in this collection (see also pp. 31 and 69), and all are sinewy physical expressions of metaphysical theology. All three, in fact, combine direct address with strong imperative verbs, devices that add immediacy and drama.

Donne says, "Death, be not proud" and "Batter my heart, three-personed God," and here addresses the trumpet-sounding angels *and* the souls of the dead and the deathless worthies *and* the Lord.

We can glimpse here something of the Metaphysical poets' fondness for paradox and education: this poet knows that the earth is round and its "corners" merely imaginary; he also knows that angels are not bound by literal laws of physics. They, like the vernacular today, still observe "the four corners of the world."

At the Round Earth's Imagined Corners

At the round earth's imagined corners, blow
Your trumpets, angels, and arise, arise
From death, you numberless infinities
Of souls, and to your scattered bodies go,
All whom the flood did, and fire shall o'erthrow,
All whom war, dearth, age, agues, tyrannies,
Despair, law, chance, hath slain, and you whose eyes,
Shall behold God, and never taste death's woe.
But let them sleep, Lord, and me mourn a space,
For, if above all these, my sins abound,
'Tis late to ask abundance of thy grace,
When we are there; here on this lowly ground,
Teach me how to repent; for that's as good
As if thou hadst sealed my pardon, with thy blood.

81

VIRTUE

~

George Herbert

---

*I*t is nothing special for a clergyman such as Herbert to entitle poems "Love" (p. 71) and "Virtue"; to write such poems so successfully, however, that they qualify for inclusion three hundred and fifty years later in an anthology of great poems—that is a true achievement.

As Louis Martz has observed, "Virtue" is constructed according to a deepening of the meaning of "sweet," progressing from the simple sensual pleasure (in Herbert's day as much a matter of smell as of taste) to a moral asset of the soul.

Virtue

Sweet day, so cool, so calm, so bright,
The bridal of the earth and sky:
The dew shall weep thy fall tonight;
    For thou must die.

Sweet rose, whose hue angry and brave
Bids the rash gazer wipe his eye:
Thy root is ever in its grave,
    And thou must die.

Sweet spring, full of sweet days and roses,
A box where sweets compacted lie;
My music shows ye have your closes,
    And all must die.

Only a sweet and virtuous soul,
Like seasoned timber, never gives;
But though the whole world turn to coal,
    Then chiefly lives.

82

ASK ME NO MORE WHERE JOVE BESTOWS

~

Thomas Carew

As with John Donne and others of the Metaphysical school, Carew offers the reader a combination of erotic lyric grace and elaborate intellectual showing-off.

The "causes" here come from Aristotle's philosophy, in which anything is the result of the operation of four causes: the final cause (purpose), the formal cause (size, shape, form), the material cause (matter), and the efficient cause (maker and process of making). Things inhere in their causes; so roses may be said to "sleep" in their causes and, by a fancy extension of meaning, to sleep as well in the addressee's beauty. "Dividing" is a technical term in music; "atom" in Carew's day meant an indivisible particle (the word, in fact, means "uncuttable," so our modern atom-splitting violates the spirit of its etymology).

Ask Me No More Where Jove Bestows

Ask me no more where Jove bestows,
When June is past, the fading rose;
For in your beauty's orient deep
These flowers, as in their causes, sleep.

Ask me no more whither do stray
The golden atoms of the day;
For in pure love heaven did prepare
Those powders to enrich your hair.

Ask me no more whither doth haste
The nightingale when May is past,
For in your sweet dividing throat
She winters, and keeps warm her note.

Ask me no more where those stars light
That downwards fall in dead of night,
For in your eyes they sit, and there
Fixed become, as in their sphere.

Ask me no more if east or west
The phoenix builds her spicy nest,
For unto you at last she flies
And in your fragrant bosom dies.

83

ODE ON THE DEATH OF A FAVORITE CAT, DROWNED IN A TUB OF GOLD FISHES

~

Thomas Gray

Gray's "Ode" and his "Elegy Written in a Country Churchyard" (p. 40) display perhaps a greater range of styles than any other set of poems by the same poet in this collection. The "Elegy" is somber, dark, and earnest; this poem is flippant and airy.

It belongs to the family of animal fables whose pedigree goes back to Aesop and, beyond that, to the Pleistocene (and—who knows?—comes forward to the bestiary preserved in cartoons of every sort).

There are pedants whose chief recreation lies in pointing out, ever so patronizingly and disdainfully, that the Bible does not say "sweat of your brow" or "gild the lily" or "spare the rod and spoil the child" or whatever; even in their sleep they murmur "Under *a* spreading chestnut tree" and " 'Twas the night before Christmas *when* all through," etc. This poem is a favorite of theirs (and, blush, mine) on account of the "glisters" in the last line (not "glitters," you ninny).

The cat in question belonged to the estimable Horace Walpole.

Ode on the Death of a Favorite Cat, Drowned in a Tub of Gold Fishes

'Twas on a lofty vase's side,
    Where China's gayest art had dyed
  The azure flowers that blow;
Demurest of the tabby kind,
The pensive Selima reclined,
    Gazed on the lake below.

Her conscious tail her joy declared;
The fair round face, the snowy beard,
    The velvet of her paws,
Her coat, that with the tortoise vies,
Her ears of jet, and emerald eyes,
    She saw; and purr'd applause.

Still had she gazed; but 'midst the tide
Two angel forms were seen to glide,
    The Genii of the stream:
Their scaly armor's Tyrian hue
Thro' richest purple to the view
    Betray'd a golden gleam.

The hapless Nymph with wonder saw:
A whisker first and then a claw,
    With many an ardent wish,
She stretch'd in vain to reach the prize.
What female heart can gold despise?
    What Cat's averse to fish?
Presumptuous Maid! with looks intent
Again she stretch'd, again she bent,
    Nor knew the gulf between.
(Malignant Fate sat by, and smil'd)
The slipp'ry verge her feet beguil'd,
    She tumbled headlong in.

Eight times emerging from the flood
She mew'd to ev'ry watry God,
    Some speedy aid to send.
No Dolphin came, no Nereid stirr'd:
Nor cruel *Tom,* nor *Susan* heard.
    A Fav'rite has no friend!

From hence, ye Beauties, undeceiv'd,
Know, one false step is ne'er retriev'd,
    And be with caution bold.
Not all that tempts your wand'ring eyes
And heedless hearts, is lawful prize;
    Nor all, that glisters, gold.

84

THE RIME OF THE
ANCIENT MARINER

~

Samuel Taylor Coleridge

---

*P*oetry, according to the brilliant Chapter XIV of Coleridge's *Biographia Literaria,* draws energy from the imagination, a power that "reveals itself in the balance or reconciliation of opposite or discordant qualities." Coleridge then lists a sampling of these balanced qualities: sameness, difference; generality, concreteness; idea, image; individuality, representativeness; novelty, familiarity; judgment, enthusiasm; naturalness, artificiality; "a more than usual state of emotion, with more than usual order."

One could appeal to this set of insights as a way of explaining some of the hypnotic power of "The Rime of the Ancient Mariner," which is at once a fascinating adventure story and a parabolical analysis of ethics; a long poem and an economical narrative; a sober tragedy but also, being told by the mariner to a wedding guest, a jubilant epithalamium; a recalling and recounting of immemorial hauntings and myth-makings *and* a present-tense realization of absolute immediacy, beginning "It is . . . ."

The Rime of the Ancient Mariner

IN SEVEN PARTS

Facile credo, plures esse Naturas invisibiles quam visibiles in rerum universitate. Sed horum [sic] omnium familiam quis nobis enarrabit? et gradus et cognationes et discrimina et singulorum munera? Quid agunt? quae loca habitant? Harum rerum notitiam semper ambivit ingenium humanum, nunquam attigit. Juvat, inverea, non diffiteor, quandoque, in animo, in tabulâ, majoris et melioris mundi imaginem contemplari: ne mens assuefacta hodiernae vitae minutiis se contrahat nimis, et tota subsidat in pusillas cogitationes. Sed veritati interea invigilandum est, modusque servandus, ut certa ab incertis, diem a nocte, distinguamus. —T. BURNET

PART I

An ancient Mariner meeteth three Gallants bidden to a wedding feast, and detaineth one.

It is an ancient Mariner
And he stoppeth one of three.
—"By thy long gray beard and glittering eye,
Now wherefore stopp'st thou me?

The Bridegroom's doors are opened wide,
And I am next of kin;
The guests are met, the feast is set:
May'st hear the merry din."

He holds him with his skinny hand,
"There was a ship," quoth he.
"Hold off! unhand me, graybeard loon!"
Eftsoons his hand dropped he.

The Wedding Guest is
spellbound by the eye of
the old seafaring man,
and constrained to hear
his tale.

He holds him with his glittering eye—
The Wedding Guest stood still,
And listens like a three years' child:
The Mariner hath his will.

The Wedding Guest sat on a stone:
He cannot choose but hear;
And thus spake on that ancient man,
The bright-eyed Mariner.

"The ship was cheered, the harbor cleared,
Merrily did we drop
Below the kirk, below the hill,
Below the lighthouse top.

The Mariner tells how
the ship sailed southward
with a good wind and
fair weather, till it
reached the line.

The Sun came up upon the left,
Out of the sea came he!
And he shone bright, and on the right
Went down into the sea.

Higher and higher every day,
Till over the mast at noon—"
The Wedding Guest here beat his breast,
For he heard the loud bassoon.

The Wedding Guest
heareth the bridal music;
but the Mariner
continueth his tale.

The bride hath placed into the hall,
Red as a rose is she;
Nodding their heads before her goes
The merry minstrelsy.

The Wedding Guest he beat his breast,
Yet he cannot choose but hear;
And thus spake on that ancient man,
The bright-eyed Mariner.

The ship driven by a
storm toward the South
Pole.

"And now the STORM-BLAST came and he
Was tyrannous and strong;
He struck with his o'ertaking wings,
And chased us south along.

With sloping masts and dipping prow,
As who pursued with yell and blow
Still treads the shadow of his foe,
And forward bends his head,
The ship drove fast, loud roared the blast,
And southward aye we fled.

And now there came both mist and snow,
And it grew wondrous cold:
And ice, mast-high, came floating by,
As green as emerald.

The land of ice, and of
fearful sounds where no
living thing was to be
seen.

And through the drifts the snowy clifts
Did send a dismal sheen:
Nor shapes of men nor beasts we ken—
The ice was all between.

The ice was here, the ice was there,
The ice was all around:
It cracked and growled, and roared and howled,
Like noises in a swound!

Till a great sea bird,
called the Albatross, came
through the snow-fog,
and was received with
great joy and hospitality.

At length did cross an Albatross,
Thorough the fog it came;
As if it had been a Christian soul,
We hailed it in God's name.

It ate the food it ne'er had eat,
And round and round it flew.
The ice did split with a thunder-fit;
The helmsman steered us through!

And lo! the Albatross
proveth a bird of good
omen, and followeth the
ship as it returned
northward through fog
and floating ice.

And a good south wind sprung up behind;
The Albatross did follow,
And every day, for food or play,
Came to the mariners' hollo!

In mist or cloud, on mast or shroud,
It perched for vespers nine;
Whiles all the night, through fog-smoke white,
Glimmered the white Moon-shine."

The ancient Mariner inhospitably killeth the pious bird of good omen.

"God save thee, ancient Mariner!
From the fiends, that plague thee thus!—
Why look'st thou so?"—With my crossbow
I shot the ALBATROSS.

PART II

The Sun now rose upon the right:
Out of the sea came he,
Still hid in mist, and on the left
Went down into the sea.

And the good south wind still blew behind,
But no sweet bird did follow,
Nor any day for food or play
Came to the mariners' hollo!

His shipmates cry out against the ancient Mariner, for killing the bird of good luck.

And I had done a hellish thing,
And it would work 'em woe:
For all averred, I had killed the bird
That made the breeze to blow.
Ah wretch! said they, the bird to slay,
That made the breeze to blow!

But when the fog cleared off, they justify the same, and thus make themselves accomplices in the crime.

Nor dim nor red, like God's own head,
The glorious Sun uprist:
Then all averred, I had killed the bird
That brought the fog and mist.
'Twas right, said they, such birds to slay,
That bring the fog and mist.

The fair breeze continues; the ship enters the Pacific Ocean, and sails northward, even till it reaches the Line.

The fair breeze blew, the white foam flew,
The furrow followed free;
We were the first that ever burst
Into that silent sea.

The ship hath been
suddenly becalmed.

Down dropped the breeze, the sails dropped
  down,
'Twas sad as sad could be;
And we did speak only to break
The silence of the sea!

All in a hot and copper sky,
The bloody Sun, at noon,
Right up above the mist did stand,
No bigger than the Moon.

Day after day, day after day,
We stuck, nor breath nor motion;
As idle as a painted ship
Upon a painted ocean.

And the Albatross begins
to be avenged.

Water, water, everywhere,
And all the boards did shrink;
Water, water, everywhere,
Nor any drop to drink.

The very deep did rot: O Christ!
That ever this should be!
Yea, slimy things did crawl with legs
Upon the slimy sea.

About, about, in reel and rout
The death-fires danced at night;
The water, like a witch's oils,
Burnt green, and blue and white.

And some in dreams assuréd were
Of the Spirit that plagued us so;
Nine fathom deep he had followed us
From the land of mist and snow.

A Spirit had followed
them; one of the invisible
inhabitants of this planet,
neither departed souls nor
angels; concerning whom
the learned Jew, Jose-
phus, and the Platonic
Constantinopolitan,
Michael Psellus, may be
consulted. They are very
numerous, and there is
no climate or element
without one or more.

And every tongue, through utter drought,
Was withered at the root;
We could not speak, no more than if
We had been choked with soot.

The shipmates, in their
sore distress, would fain
throw the whole guilt on
the ancient Mariner: in
sign whereof they hang
the dead sea bird round
his neck.

Ah! well-a-day! what evil looks
Had I from old and young!
Instead of the cross, the Albatross
About my neck was hung.

PART III

There passed a weary time. Each throat
Was parched, and glazed each eye.
A weary time! a weary time!
How glazed each weary eye,
When looking westward, I beheld
A something in the sky.

The ancient Mariner
beholdeth a sign in the
element afar off.

At first it seemed a little speck,
And then it seemed a mist;
It moved and moved, and took at last
A certain shape, I wist.

A speck, a mist, a shape, I wist!
And still it neared and neared:
As if it dodged a water sprite,
It plunged and tacked and veered.

At its nearer approach, it
seemeth him to be a
ship; and at a dear
ransom he freeth his
speech from the bonds of
thirst.

With throats unslaked, with black lips baked,
We could nor laugh nor wail;
Through utter drought all dumb we stood!
I bit my arm, I sucked the blood,
And cried, A sail! a sail!

A flash of joy;

With throats unslaked, with black lips baked,
Agape they heard me call:
Gramercy! they for joy did grin,
And all at once their breath drew in,
As they were drinking all.

And horror follows. For
can it be a ship that
comes onward without
wind or tide?

See! see! (I cried) she tacks no more!
Hither to work us weal;
Without a breeze, without a tide,
She steadies with upright keel!

The western wave was all aflame.
The day was well nigh done!
Almost upon the western wave
Rested the broad bright Sun;
When that strange shape drove suddenly
Betwixt us and the Sun.

It seemeth him but the
skeleton of a ship.

And straight the Sun was flecked with bars,
(Heaven's Mother send us grace!)
As if through a dungeon grate he peered
With broad and burning face.

Alas! (thought I, and my heart beat loud)

And its ribs are seen as
bars on the face of the
setting Sun.

How fast she nears and nears!
Are those *her* sails that glance in the Sun,
Like restless gossameres?

The Specter-Woman and
her Deathmate, and no
other on board the
skeleton ship.

Are those *her* ribs through which the Sun
Did peer, as through a grate?
And is that Woman all her crew?
Is that a DEATH? and are there two?
Is DEATH that woman's mate?

Like vessel, like crew!

Her lips were red, *her* looks were free,
Her locks were yellow as gold:
Her skin was as white as leprosy,
The Nightmare LIFE-IN-DEATH was she,
Who thicks man's blood with cold.

Death and Life-in-Death
have diced for the ship's
crew, and she (the latter)
winneth the ancient
Mariner.

The naked hulk alongside came,
And the twain were casting dice;
"The game is done! I've won! I've won!"
Quoth she, and whistles thrice.

No twilight within the
courts of the Sun.

The Sun's rim dips; the stars rush out:
At one stride comes the dark;
With far-heard whisper, o'er the sea,
Off shot the specter-bark.

At the rising of the
Moon,

We listened and looked sideways up!
Fear at my heart, as at a cup,
My lifeblood seemed to sip!
The stars were dim, and thick the night,

The steersman's face by his lamp gleamed white;
From the sails the dew did drip—
Till clomb above the eastern bar
The hornéd Moon, with one bright star
Within the nether tip.

One after another,

One after one, by the star-dogged Moon,
Too quick for groan or sigh,
Each turned his face with ghastly pang,
And cursed me with his eye.

His shipmates drop down dead.

Four times fifty living men,
(And I heard nor sigh nor groan)
With heavy thump, a lifeless lump,
They dropped down one by one.

But Life-in-Death begins her work on the ancient Mariner.

The souls did from their bodies fly—
They fled to bliss or woe!
And every soul, it passed me by,
Like the whizz of my cross-bow!

PART IV

The Wedding Guest feareth that a Spirit is talking to him;

"I fear thee, ancient Mariner!
I fear thy skinny hand!
And thou art long, and lank, and brown,
As is the ribbed sea-sand.

I fear thee and thy glittering eye,
And thy skinny hand, so brown."—

But the ancient Mariner assureth him of his bodily life, and proceedeth to relate his horrible penance.

Fear not, fear not, thou Wedding Guest!
This body dropped not down.

Alone, alone, all, all alone,
Alone on a wide wide sea!
And never a saint took pity on
My soul in agony.

He despiseth the creatures of the calm,

The many men, so beautiful!
And they all dead did lie:
And a thousand thousand slimy things
Lived on; and so did I.

And envieth that they should live, and so many lie dead.

I looked upon the rotting sea,
And drew my eyes away;
I looked upon the rotting deck,
And there the dead men lay.

I looked to heaven, and tried to pray;
But or ever a prayer had gushed,
A wicked whisper came, and made
My heart as dry as dust.

I closed my lids, and kept them close,
And the balls like pulses beat,
For the sky and the sea, and the sea and the sky
Lay like a load on my weary eye,
And the dead were at my feet.

But the curse liveth for him in the eye of the dead men.

The cold sweat melted from their limbs,
Nor rot nor reek did they:
The look with which they looked on me
Had never passed away.

An orphan's curse would drag to hell
A spirit from on high;
But oh! more horrible than that
Is the curse in a dead man's eye!
Seven days, seven nights, I saw that curse,
And yet I could not die.

The moving Moon went up the sky,
And nowhere did abide;
Softly she was going up,
And a star or two beside—

In his loneliness and fixedness he yearneth towards the journeying Moon, and the stars that still sojourn, yet still move onward; and everywhere the blue sky belongs to them, and is their appointed rest, and their native country and their own natural homes, which they enter unannounced, as lords that are certainly

Her beams bemocked the sultry main,
Like April hoar-frost spread;
But where the ship's huge shadow lay,
The charméd water burnt alway
A still and awful red.

*expected and yet there is
a silent joy at their
arrival.*

*By the light of the Moon
he beholdeth God's
creatures of the great
calm.*

Beyond the shadow of the ship,
I watched the water snakes:
They moved in tracks of shining white,
And when they reared, the elfish light
Fell off in hoary flakes.

Within the shadow of the ship
I watched their rich attire:
Blue, glossy green, and velvet black,
They coiled and swam; and every track
Was a flash of golden fire.

*Their beauty and their
happiness.*

O happy living things! no tongue
Their beauty might declare:
A spring of love gushed from my heart,

*He blesseth them in his
heart.*

And I blessed them unaware:
Sure my kind saint took pity on me,
And I blessed them unaware.

*The spell begins to
break.*

The self-same moment I could pray;
And from my neck so free
The Albatross fell off, and sank
Like lead into the sea.

PART V

Oh sleep! it is a gentle thing,
Beloved from pole to pole!
To Mary Queen the praise be given!
She sent the gentle sleep from Heaven,
That slid into my soul.

*Be grace of the holy
Mother, the ancient
Mariner is refreshed with
rain.*

The silly buckets on the deck,
That had so long remained,
I dreamt that they were filled with dew;
And when I awoke, it rained.

My lips were wet, my throat was cold,
My garments all were dank;

Sure I had drunken in my dreams,
And still my body drank.

I moved, and could not feel my limbs;
I was so light—almost
I thought that I had died in sleep,
And was a blessèd ghost.

He heareth sounds and
seeth strange sights and
commotions in the sky
and the element.

And soon I heard a roaring wind:
It did not come anear;
But with its sound it shook the sails,
That were so thin and sere.

The upper air burst into life!
And a hundred fire-flags sheen,
To and fro they were hurried about!
And to and fro, and in and out,
The wan stars danced between.

And the coming wind did roar more loud,
And the sails did sigh like sedge;
And the rain poured down from one black cloud;
The Moon was at its edge.

The thick black cloud was cleft, and still
The Moon was at its side:
Like waters shot from some high crag,
The lightning fell with never a jag,
A river steep and wide.

The bodies of the ship's
crew are inspirited, and
the ship moves on;

The loud wind never reached the ship,
Yet now the ship moved on!
Beneath the lightning and the Moon
The dead men gave a groan.

They groaned, they stirred, they all uprose,
Nor spake, nor moved their eyes;
It had been strange, even in a dream,
To have seen those dead men rise.

The helmsman steered, the ship moved on;
Yet never a breeze up-blew;
The mariners all 'gan work the ropes,

Where they were wont to do;
They raised their limbs like lifeless tools—
We were a ghastly crew.

The body of my brother's son
Stood by me, knee to knee:
The body and I pulled at one rope,
But he said nought to me.

But not by the souls of
the men, nor by demons
of earth or middle air,
but by a blessèd troop of.
angelic spirits, sent down
by the invocation of the
guardian saint.

"I fear thee, ancient Mariner!"
Be calm, thou Wedding Guest!
'Twas not those souls that fled in pain,
Which to their corses came again,
But a troop of spirits blest:

For when it dawned—they dropped their arms,
And clustered round the mast;
Sweet sounds rose slowly through their mouths,
And from their bodies passed.

Around, around, flew each sweet sound,
Then darted to the Sun;
Slowly the sounds came back again,
Now mixed, now one by one.

Sometimes a-dropping from the sky
I heard the sky-lark sing;
Sometimes all little birds that are,
How they seemed to fill the sea and air
With their sweet jargoning!

And now 'twas like all instruments,
Now like a lonely flute;
And now it is an angel's song,
That makes the heavens be mute.

It ceased; yet still the sails made on
A pleasant noise till noon,
A noise like of a hidden brook
In the leafy month of June,
That to the sleeping woods all night
Singeth a quiet tune.

Till noon we quietly sailed on,
Yet never a breeze did breathe:
Slowly and smoothly went the ship,
Moved onward from beneath.

Under the keel nine fathom deep,
From the land of mist and snow,
The spirit slid: and it was he
That made the ship to go.
The sails at noon left off their tune,
And the ship stood still also.

The Sun, right up above the mast,
Had fixed her to the ocean:
But in a minute she 'gan stir,
With a short uneasy motion—
Backwards and forwards half her length
With a short uneasy motion.

Then like a pawing horse let go,
She made a sudden bound:
It flung the blood into my head,
And I fell down in a swound.

How long in that same fit I lay,
I have not to declare;
But ere my living life returned,
I heard and in my soul discerned
Two voices in the air.

"Is it he?" quoth one, "Is this the man?
By him who died on cross,
With his cruel bow he laid full low
The harmless Albatross.

The spirit who bideth by himself
In the land of mist and snow,
He loved the bird that loved the man
Who shot him with his bow."

The other was a softer voice,
As soft as honey-dew:
Quoth he, "The man hath penance done,

And penance more will do."

PART VI

"But tell me, tell me! speak again,
Thy soft response renewing—
What makes that ship drive on so fast?
What is the ocean doing?"

"Still as a slave before his lord,
The ocean hath no blast;
His great bright eye most silently
Up to the Moon is cast—

If he may know which way to go;
For she guides him smooth or grim.
See, brother, see! how graciously
She looketh down on him."

The Mariner hath been cast into a trance; for the angelic power causeth the vessel to drive northward faster than human life could endure.

"But why drives on that ship so fast,
Without or wave or wind?"

"The air is cut away before,
And closes from behind.

Fly, brother, fly! more high, more high!
Or we shall be belated:
For slow and slow that ship will go,
When the Mariner's trance is abated."

The supernatural motion is retarded; the Mariner awakes, and his penance begins anew.

I woke, and we were sailing on
As in a gentle weather:
'Twas night, calm night, the moon was high;
The dead men stood together.

174 ~ THE RIME OF THE ANCIENT MARINER

All stood together on the deck,
For a charnel-dungeon fitter:
All fixed on me their stony eyes,
That in the Moon did glitter.

The pang, the curse, with which they died,
Had never passed away:
I could not draw my eyes from theirs,
Nor turn them up to pray.

The curse is finally expiated.

And now this spell was snapped: once more
I viewed the ocean green,
And looked far forth, yet little saw
Of what had else been seen—

Like one, that on a lonesome road
Doth walk in fear and dread,
And having once turned round walks on,
And turns no more his head;
Because he knows, a frightful fiend
Doth close behind him tread.

But soon there breathed a wind on me,
Nor sound nor motion made:
Its path was not upon the sea,
In ripple or in shade.

It raised my hair, it fanned my cheek
Like a meadow-gale of spring—
It mingled strangely with my fears,
Yet it felt like a welcoming.

Swiftly, swiftly flew the ship,
Yet she sailed softly too:
Sweetly, sweetly blew the breeze—
On me alone it blew.

And the ancient Mariner beholdeth his native country.

Oh! dream of joy! is this indeed
The lighthouse top I see?
Is this the hill? is this the kirk?
Is this mine own countree?

We drifted o'er the harbor-bar,

And I with sobs did pray—
O let me be awake, my God!
Or let me sleep alway.

The harbor-bay was clear as glass,
So smoothly it was strewn!
And on the bay the moonlight lay,
And the shadow of the Moon.

The rock shone bright, the kirk no less,
That stands above the rock:
The moonlight steeped in silentness
The steady weathercock.

The angelic spirits leave
the dead bodies,

And the bay was white with silent light,
Till rising from the same,
Full many shapes, that shadows were,
In crimson colors came.

A little distance from the prow
Those crimson shadows were:
And appear in their own
forms of light.
I turned my eyes upon the deck—
Oh, Christ! what saw I there!

Each corse lay flat, lifeless and flat,
And, by the holy rood!
A man all light, a seraph-man,
On every corse there stood.

This seraph-band, each waved his hand:
It was a heavenly sight!
They stood as signals to the land,
Each one a lovely light;

This seraph-band, each waved his hand,
No voice did they impart—
No voice; but oh! the silence sank
Like music on my heart.

But soon I heard the dash of oars,
I heard the Pilot's cheer;
My head was turned perforce away
And I saw a boat appear.

The Pilot and the Pilot's boy,
I heard them coming fast:
Dear Lord in Heaven! it was a joy
The dead men could not blast.

I saw a third—I heard his voice:
It is the Hermit good!
He singeth loud his godly hymns
That he makes in the wood.
He'll shrieve my soul, he'll wash away
The Albatross's blood.

PART VII

The Hermit of the Wood

This Hermit good lives in that wood
Which slopes down to the sea.
How loudly his sweet voice he rears!
He loves to talk with marineres
That come from a far countree.

He kneels at morn, and noon, and eve—
He hath a cushion plump:
It is the moss that wholly hides
The rotted old oak stump.

The skiff-boat neared: I heard them talk,
"Why, this is strange, I trow!
Where are those lights so many and fair,
That signal made but now?"

Approacheth the ship
with wonder.

"Strange, by my faith!" the Hermit said—
"And they answered not our cheer!
The planks looked warped! and see those sails,
How thin they are and sere!
I never saw aught like to them,
Unless perchance it were

Brown skeletons of leaves that lag
My forest-brook along;
When the ivy tod is heavy with snow,
And the owlet whoops to the wolf below,
That eats the she-wolf's young."

"Dear Lord! it hath a fiendish look,"
The Pilot made reply,
"I am a-feared"—"Push on, push on!"
Said the Hermit cheerily.

The boat came closer to the ship,
But I nor spake nor stirred;
The boat came close beneath the ship,
And straight a sound was heard.

The ship suddenly
sinketh.

Under the water it rumbled on,
Still louder and more dread:
It reached the ship, it split the bay;
The ship went down like lead.

The ancient Mariner is
saved in the Pilot's boat.

Stunned by that loud and dreadful sound,
Which sky and ocean smote,
Like one that hath been seven days drowned
My body lay afloat;
But swift as dreams, myself I found
Within the Pilot's boat.

Upon the whirl, where sank the ship,
The boat spun round and round;
And all was still, save that the hill
Was telling of the sound.

I moved my lips—the Pilot shrieked
And fell down in a fit;
The holy Hermit raised his eyes,
And prayed where he did sit.

I took the oars: the Pilot's boy,
Who now doth crazy go,
Laughed loud and long, and all the while
His eyes went to and fro.
"Ha! ha!" quoth he, "full plain I see,
The Devil knows how to row."

And now, all in my own countree,
I stood on the firm land!
The Hermit stepped forth from the boat,
And scarcely he could stand.

The ancient Mariner
earnestly entreateth the
Hermit to shrieve him;
and the penance of life
falls on him.

"O shrieve me, shrieve me, holy man!"
The Hermit crossed his brow.
"Say quick," quoth he, "I bid thee say—
What manner of man art thou?"

Forthwith this frame of mine was wrenched
With a woeful agony,
Which forced me to begin my tale;
And then it left me free.

And ever and anon
throughout his future life
an agony constraineth
him to travel from land
to land;

Since then, at an uncertain hour,
That agony returns:
And till my ghastly tale is told,
This heart within me burns.

I pass, like night, from land to land;
I have strange power of speech;
That moment that his face I see,
I know the man that must hear me:
To him my tale I teach.

What loud uproar bursts from the door!
The wedding guests are there:
But in the garden-bower the bride
And bridemaids singing are:
And hark the little vesper bell,
Which biddeth me to prayer!

O Wedding Guest! this soul hath been
Alone on a wide wide sea:
So lonely 'twas, that God himself
Scarce seeméd there to be.

O sweeter than the marriage feast,
'Tis sweeter far to me,
To walk together to the kirk
With a goodly company!

To walk together to the kirk,
And all together pray,
While each to his great Father bends,
Old men, and babes, and loving friends
And youths and maidens gay!

Farewell, farewell! but this I tell
To thee, thou Wedding Guest!
He prayeth well, who loveth well
Both man and bird and beast.

He prayeth best, who loveth best
All things both great and small;
For the dear God who loveth us,
He made and loveth all.

The Mariner, whose eye is bright,
Whose beard with age is hoar,
Is gone: and now the Wedding Guest
Turned from the bridegroom's door.

He went like one that hath been stunned,
And is of sense forlorn:
A sadder and a wiser man,
He rose the morrow morn.

85

CONCORD HYMN

~

Ralph Waldo Emerson

*I*t is unlikely that Emerson the transcendentalist, mystic, and advocate of free verse would choose the "Concord Hymn" as the only representative of his work for an anthology; and the poem indeed does seem to survive almost in spite of itself, an occasional poem that has so strongly survived its occasion that many readers will not know which Concord is involved (the one in New Hampshire? in Massachusetts? one of the seven in North Carolina?) or why. And many, like me, will not be able to recall any of the stanzas beyond the first, on which all of the poem's fame relies.

Concord Hymn

Sung at the completion of the Battle Monument,
July 4, 1837

By the rude bridge that arched the flood,
   Their flag to April's breeze unfurled,
Here once the embattled farmers stood
   And fired the shot heard round the world.

The foe long since in silence slept;
   Alike the conqueror silent sleeps;
And Time the ruined bridge has swept
   Down the dark stream which seaward creeps.

On this green bank, by this soft stream,
   We set to-day a votive stone;
That memory may their deed redeem,
   When, like our sires, our sons are gone.

Spirit, that made those heroes dare
   To die, and leave their children free,
Bid Time and Nature gently spare
   The shaft we raise to them and thee.

86

THE LAKE ISLE OF INNISFREE

~

William Butler Yeats

Yeat's celebrated poem of nostalgia was apparently inspired—not by genuine desire to lead a simple agricultural life—but by falling asleep over Thoreau's *Walden*. It has been observed that anyone who says inverted things like "And a small cabin build there, of clay and wattles made" will never be a success as bean-farmer and beekeeper.

Yeats's rather ingenuous lyric provoked two responses by Ezra Pound (in "Mauberley" and "The Lake Isle"), one by William Carlos Williams ("These"), and one by Wallace Stevens ("Page from a Tale").

As you may know from the John Wayne movie *The Quiet Man,* the place-name is pronounced "Innishfree."

The Lake Isle of Innisfree

I will arise and go now, and go to Innisfree,
And a small cabin build there, of clay and wattles made:
Nine bean-rows will I have there, a hive for the honey-bee,
And live alone in the bee-loud glade.

And I shall have some peace there, for peace comes dropping slow,
Dropping from the veils of the morning to where the cricket sings;
There midnight's all a glimmer, and noon a purple glow,
And evening full of the linnet's wings.

I will arise and go now, for always night and day
I hear lake water lapping with low sounds by the shore;
While I stand on the roadway, or on the pavements gray,
I hear it in the deep heart's core.

87

NON SUM QUALIS ERAM BONAE SUB REGNO CYNARAE

~

Ernest Dowson

*F*rom Horace's *Odes* I.iv: "I am not what I was under the rule of the kind Cynara."

Another of Dowson's Latin-titled poems ("Vitae Summa Brevis Spem Nos Vetat Incohare Longam") furnishes *Days of Wine and Roses;* this seemingly modest poem provides the model of a memorable Cole Porter song ("Always true to you, darlin', in my fashion") and the phrase "Gone with the wind" that turns up in James Joyce's *Ulysses* and elsewhere. Dowson's poem even contributes a phrase to T. S. Eliot's "The Hollow Men" (about a shadow falling).

Non Sum Qualis Eram Bonae sub Regno Cynarae

Last night, ah, yesternight, betwixt her lips and mine
There fell thy shadow, Cynara! thy breath was shed
Upon my soul between the kisses and the wine;
And I was desolate and sick of an old passion,
    Yea, I was desolate and bowed my head:
I have been faithful to thee, Cynara! in my fashion.

All night upon mine heart I felt her warm heart beat,
Night-long within mine arms in love and sleep she lay;
Surely the kisses of her bought red mouth were sweet;
But I was desolate and sick of an old passion,
    When I awoke and found the dawn was gray:
I have been faithful to thee, Cynara! in my fashion.

I have forgot much, Cynara! gone with the wind,
Flung roses, roses riotously with the throng,
Dancing, to put thy pale, lost lilies out of mind;
But I was desolate and sick of an old passion,
    Yea, all the time, because the dance was long:
I have been faithful to thee, Cynara! in my fashion.

I cried for madder music and for stronger wine,
But when the feast is finished and the lamps expire,
Then falls thy shadow, Cynara! the night is thine;
And I am desolate and sick of an old passion,
   Yea, hungry for the lips of my desire:
I have been faithful to thee, Cynara! in my fashion.

88

MY PAPA'S WALTZ

~

Theodore Roethke

Roethke, Kenneth Rexroth (born in 1905), and several others in the same generation grew up during Prohibition and had, for better or worse (usually the latter), a love-hate relationship with alcoholism—parental, personal, or both.

Roethke was descended from a long line of Prussian horticulturists (foresters, nurserymen, and suchlike). The papa here is a complex peasant, drunk and dancing, in a "waltz" that is somehow not a comfortable waltz; the poem is an expression of affection that also suggests fear and death, but is, after all, humorous and loving.

John Frederick Nims has pointed out that the waltz (a dance in three-four time) is rendered in this poem with lines of three stresses.

My Papa's Waltz

The whiskey on your breath
Could make a small boy dizzy;
But I hung on like death:
Such waltzing was not easy.

We romped until the pans
Slid from the kitchen shelf;
My mother's countenance
Could not unfrown itself.

The hand that held my wrist
Was battered on one knuckle;
At every step you missed
My right ear scraped a buckle.

You beat time on my head
With a palm caked hard by dirt,
Then waltzed me off to bed
Still clinging to your shirt.

89

THE NYMPH'S REPLY TO
THE SHEPHERD

~

Sir Walter Ralegh

*I*t is probable but not certain that Ralegh wrote this reply to Marlowe's "The Passionate Shepherd to His Love" (p. 29); see that poem for more commentary on this answer.

If "The Nymph's Reply" *is* by Ralegh, then he is the second-oldest named poet represented in this book. He is also among the most versatile and the only one a state capital is named for. He was a courtier and politician, and his presence as the author of a response to another poet's work says something about the community of letters, which, to dragoon some passing critical catchwords, is more often dialogic than monologic and shows more intertextual heteroglossia in a carnivalesque spirit of play and debate than simple unilateral expression of easy emotions.

The Nymph's Reply to
the Shepherd

If all the world and love were young,
And truth in every shepherd's tongue,
These pretty pleasures might me move
To live with thee and be thy Love.

But Time drives flocks from field to fold;
When rivers rage and rocks grow cold;
And Philomel becometh dumb;
The rest complains of cares to come.

The flowers do fade, and wanton fields
To wayward Winter reckoning yields:
A honey tongue, a heart of gall,
Is fancy's spring, but sorrow's fall.

Thy gowns, thy shoes, thy beds of roses,
Thy cap, thy kirtle, and thy posies,
Soon break, soon wither—soon forgotten,
In folly ripe, in reason rotten.

Thy belt of straw and ivy-buds,
Thy coral clasps and amber studs,—
All these in me no means can move
To come to thee and be thy Love.

But could youth last, and love still breed,
Had joys no date, nor age no need,
Then these delights my mind might move
To live with thee and be thy Love.

90

GO AND CATCH A FALLING STAR

~

John Donne

Like many of Donne's "Holy Sonnets," this poem begins with a robust series of imperatives: do this and this impossible thing. The series is more or less conventional, but the items are joined by certain dark underlying similarities (the devil is a sort of falling star, the mandrake root is supposedly anthropomorphic); conceivably, the prevalence of dishonesty and inconstancy is a result of the Fall.

But these love paradoxes are much less serious than the religious paradoxes much more deeply registered in the "Holy Sonnets," and it would be fatuous to pester a merry Metaphysical exercise with much ingenuity.

Go and Catch a Falling Star

Go and catch a falling star,
    Get with child a mandrake root,
Tell me where all past years are,
    Or who cleft the Devil's foot,
Teach me to hear mermaids singing,
Or to keep off envy's stinging,
        And find
        What wind
Serves to advance an honest mind.

If thou beest born to strange sights,
    Things invisible to see,
Ride ten thousand days and nights,
    Till age snow white hairs on thee.
Thou, when thou return'st, wilt tell me
All strange wonders that befell thee,
        And swear
        Nowhere
Lives a woman true, and fair.

If thou find'st one, let me know,
  Such a pilgrimage were sweet;
Yet do not, I would not go,
  Though at next door we might meet;
Though she were true when you met her,
And last till you write your letter,
          Yet she
          Will be
False, ere I come, to two, or three.

91

THE SUN RISING

~

John Donne

Here, as in the three "Holy Sonnets" of Donne's that are in this collection (pp. 31, 69, and 155), the poet avoids talking about abstractions. Instead, he gives the concept a local habitation and a name (in this case, time is situated in the sun, which is then personified as a fool and a wretch) and then talks *to* it, in imperatives, not about it.

As anyone can see, the operative strategy throughout is hyperbole—extreme exaggeration. How does Donne manage to bring it off so convincingly? Part of the answer is in the authority of his management of diction and verse; another part in his display of more-than-casual knowledge of science—in this case, astronomy and geometry.

One might compare the playful overstatement here (about the sun's mistaken self-image "so reverend and strong") with the most serious statement in Holy Sonnet X about death's mistaken self-image as "Mighty and dreadful." Donne delights in deflation of the overrated, so that the genuinely worthy—in this case, sexual love—can be praised suitably.

The Sun Rising

> Busy old fool, unruly sun,
> Why dost thou thus,
> Through windows, and through curtains call on us?
> Must to thy motions lovers' seasons run?
> Saucy pedantic wretch, go chide
> Late school-boys, and sour prentices,
> Go tell court-huntsmen, that the King will ride,
> Call country ants to harvest offices;
> Love, all alike, no season knows, nor clime,
> Nor hours, days, months, which are the rags of time.
>
> Thy beams, so reverend, and strong
> Why shouldst thou think?
> I could eclipse and cloud them with a wink,

But that I would not lose her sight so long:
  If her eyes have not blinded thine,
  Look, and tomorrow late, tell me,
 Whether both th'Indias of spice and mine
 Be where thou left'st them, or lie here with me.
Ask for those kings whom thou saw'st yesterday,
And thou shalt hear, All here in one bed lay.

  She'is all states, and all princes, I,
  Nothing else is.
Princes do but play us; compared to this,
All honor's mimic; all wealth alchemy.
  Thou sun art half as happy as we,
  In that the world's contracted thus;
 Thine age asks ease, and since thy duties be
 To warm the world, that's done in warming us.
Shine here to us, and thou art everywhere;
This bed thy center is, these walls, thy sphere.

92

LYCIDAS

~

John Milton

This is one of the great "pastoral elegies" in the language. "Pastor" originally meant "shepherd," and the fiction of pastoral elegies is that the dead subject—usually a poet—is a shepherd being lamented by another or by several others. A similar identification of poet and shepherd motivates later poets' poems about dead colleagues, most notably Shelley's "Adonais" on the death of Keats and Matthew Arnold's "Thyrsis" on the death of Arthur Hugh Clough.

The connection of poets and shepherds (also found in the Old Testament story of David) is abetted by another connection with shepherds: that of the Christian clergy, based on certain parables and expressions in the New Testament. We still say "pastoral care" today, and some readers may be aware of the irony in the title of André Gide's story *Symphonie Pastorale*.

Samuel Johnson doubted Milton's sincerity, especially in the extended pastoral metaphors and the allegory of the "ruin of our corrupted Clergy." Johnson said, "Where there is leisure for fiction there is little grief." But the poem is still read, and loved. It has provoked many volumes of commentary.

Lycidas

In this Monody the Author bewails a learned Friend, unfortunately drown'd in his passage from Chester *on the Irish Seas, 1637. And by occasion foretells the ruin of our corrupted Clergy then in their height.*

Yet once more, O ye laurels, and once more,
Ye myrtles brown, with ivy never-sere,
I come to pluck your berries harsh and crude,
And with forc'd fingers rude
Shatter your leaves before the mellowing year.
Bitter constraint and sad occasion dear
Compels me to disturb your season due:
For Lycidas is dead, dead ere his prime
Young Lycidas, and hath not left his peer.
Who would not sing for Lycidas? he well knew
Himself to sing, and build the lofty rhyme.

He must not float upon his watery bier
Unwept, and welter to the parching wind
Without the meed of some melodious tear.
   Begin then, Sisters of the sacred well
That from beneath the seat of Jove doth spring;
Begin, and somewhat loudly sweep the string:
Hence with denial vain, and coy excuse.
So may some gentle Muse
With lucky words favor my destin'd urn,
And as he passes, turn
And bid fair peace be to my sable shroud.
For we were nurs'd upon the self-same hill,
Fed the same flock, by fountain, shade and rill.
   Together both, ere the high lawns appear'd
Under the glimmering eyelids of the morn,
We drove afield, and both together heard
What time the gray-fly winds her sultry horn,
Battening our flocks with the fresh dews of night,
Oft till the ev'n-star bright
Toward heav'n's descent had slop'd his burnish'd wheel.
Meanwhile the rural ditties were not mute
Temper'd to th'oaten flute:
Rough Satyrs danc'd, and Fauns with cloven heel
From the glad sound would not be absent long,
And old Dametas lov'd to hear our song.
   But O the heavy change, now thou art gone,
Now thou art gone, and never must return!
Thee shepherd, thee the woods and desert caves
With wild thyme and the gadding vine o'ergrown
And all their echoes mourn.
The willows and the hazel copses green
Shall now no more be seen
Fanning their joyous leaves to thy soft lays.
As killing as the canker to the rose,
Or taint-worm to the weanling herds that graze,
Or frost to flowers that their gay wardrobe wear
When first the whitethorn blows,
Such, Lycidas, thy loss to shepherd's ear.
   Where were ye Nymphs when the remorseless deep
Clos'd o'er the head of your lov'd Lycidas?
For neither were ye playing on the steep,
Where your old bards the famous Druids lie,

Nor on the shaggy top of Mona high,
Nor yet where Deva spreads her wizard stream.
Ay me, I fondly dream!
Had ye been there . . . for what could that have done?
What could the Muse herself that Orpheus bore,
The Muse herself, for her enchanting son?
Whom universal nature did lament,
When by the rout that made the hideous roar
His gory visage down the stream was sent,
Down the swift Hebrus to the Lesbian shore.
   Alas! What boots it with uncessant care
To tend the homely slighted shepherd's trade,
And strictly meditate the thankless Muse?
Were it not better done as others use,
To sport with Amaryllis in the shade,
Hid in the tangles of Neaera's hair?
Fame is the spur that the clear spirit doth raise
(That last infirmity of noble mind)
To scorn delights and live laborious days;
But the fair guerdon where we hope to find,
And think to burst out into sudden blaze,
Comes the blind Fury with th'abhorred shears
And slits the thin-spun life. "But not the praise,"
Phoebus repli'd, and touch'd my trembling ears.
"Fame is no plant that grows on mortal soil,
Nor in the glistering foil
Set off to th'world, nor in broad rumor lies;
But lives, and spreads aloft by those pure eyes
And perfect witness of all-judging Jove:
As he pronounces lastly on each deed,
Of so much fame in Heav'n expect thy meed."
   O fountain Arethuse, and thou honor'd flood,
Smooth-sliding Mincius, crown'd with vocal reeds,
That strain I heard was of a higher mood.
But now my oat proceeds,
And listens to the herald of the sea
That came in Neptune's plea.
He ask'd the waves, and ask'd the felon winds,
"What hard mishap hath doom'd this gentle swain?"
And question'd every gust of rugged wings
That blows from off each beaked promontory.
They knew not of his story,

And sage Hippotades their answer brings
That not a blast was from his dungeon stray'd;
The air was calm, and on the level brine
Sleek Panope with all her sisters play'd.
It was that fatal and perfidious bark,
Built in th'eclipse, and rigg'd with curses dark,
That sunk so low that sacred head of thine.
    Next Camus (reverend sire) went footing slow,
His mantle hairy and his bonnet sedge
Inwrought with figures dim, and on the edge
Like to that sanguine flower inscrib'd with woe.
"Ah! Who hath reft" (quoth he) "my dearest pledge?"
Last came, and last did go,
The pilot of the Galilean lake.
Two massy keys he bore of metals twain
(The golden opes, the iron shuts amain).
He shook his mitr'd locks, and stern bespake:
"How well could I have spar'd for thee, young swain,
Enough of such as for their bellies' sake
Creep and intrude and climb into the fold?
Of other care they little reckoning make
Than how to scramble at the shearers' feast
And shove away the worthy bidden guest.
Blind mouths! that scarce themselves know how to hold
A sheephook, or have learn'd ought else the least
That to the faithful herdman's art belongs!
What recks it them? What need they? They are sped.
And when they list their lean and flashy songs
Grate on their scrannel pipes of wretched straw,
The hungry sheep look up, and are not fed,
But swoll'n with wind and the rank mist they draw,
Rot inwardly, and foul contagion spread:
Besides what the grim wolf with privy paw
Daily devours apace, and little said.
But that two-handed engine at the door
Stands ready to smite once, and smites no more."
    Return, Alpheus, the dread voice is pass'd
That shrunk thy streams; return, Sicilian Muse,
And call the vales and bid them hither cast
Their bells and flowerets of a thousand hues.
Ye valleys low, where the mild whispers use
Of shades and wanton winds and gushing brooks,

On whose fresh lap the swart star sparely looks,
Throw hither all your quaint enamel'd eyes
That on the green turf suck the honey'd showers,
And purple all the ground with vernal flowers.
Bring the rathe primrose that forsaken dies,
The tufted crow-toe and pale jessamine,
The white pink, and the pansy freak'd with jet,
The glowing violet,
The musk-rose and the well-attir'd woodbine,
With cowslips wan that hang the pensive head,
And every flower that sad embroidery wears;
Bid amaranthus all his beauty shed,
And daffodillies fill their cups with tears
To strew the laureate hearse where Lycid lies.
For so, to interpose a little ease,
Let our frail thoughts dally with false surmise;
Ay me! whilst thee the shores and sounding seas
Wash far away, where e'er thy bones are hurl'd,
Whether beyond the stormy Hebrides,
Where thou perhaps under the humming tide
Visit'st the bottom of the monstrous world,
Or whether thou, to our moist vows deni'd,
Sleep'st by the fable of Bellerus old,
Where the great vision of the guarded Mount
Looks toward Namancos and Bayona's hold.
Look homeward Angel now, and melt with ruth,
And O ye dolphins, waft the hapless youth.
    Weep no more, woeful shepherds, weep no more;
For Lycidas your sorrow is not dead,
Sunk though he be beneath the watery floor:
So sinks the daystar in the ocean bed,
And yet anon repairs his drooping head
And tricks his beams and with new-spangl'd ore
Flames in the forehead of the morning sky;
So Lycidas sunk low, but mounted high
Through the dear might of him that walk'd the waves,
Where other groves and other streams along
With nectar pure his oozy locks he laves
And hears the unexpressive nuptial song
In the bless'd kingdoms meek of joy and love.
There entertain him all the saints above

In solemn troops and sweet societies,
That sing, and singing in their glory move,
And wipe the tears for ever from his eyes.
Now, Lycidas, the shepherds weep no more.
Henceforth thou art the genius of the shore
In thy large recompense, and shalt be good
To all that wander in that perilous flood.

    Thus sang the uncouth swain to th'oaks and rills,
While the still morn went out with sandals gray;
He touch'd the tender stops of various quills,
With eager thought warbling his Doric lay.
And now the sun had stretch'd out all the hills,
And now was dropp'd into the western bay;
At last he rose, and twitch'd his mantle blue,
Tomorrow to fresh woods and pastures new.

93

TO ALTHEA, FROM PRISON

~

Richard Lovelace

*L*ovelace began with wealth, genius, amiability, and good looks but died young and poor. He was imprisoned twice for his Royalist views; he wrote this celebrated song during the first incarceration in 1642.

Many Metaphysical poems are so clever and farfetched that their wit exempts them from mundane communication; they seem to be the weightless occupations of the idle smart. Lovelace can coin memorable paradoxical phrases—

> Stone walls do not a prison make,
> Nor iron bars a cage—

but there is nothing farfetched about the sentiment; he really did do time, and his eloquence is matched only by his sincerity.

To Althea, from Prison

When Love with unconfinèd wings
  Hovers within my gates,
And my divine Althea brings
  To whisper at the grates;
When I lie tangled in her hair
  And fetter'd to her eye,
The birds that wanton in the air
  Know no such liberty.

When flowing cups run swiftly round
  With no allaying Thames,
Our careless heads with roses bound,
  Our hearts with loyal flames;
When thirsty grief in wine we steep,
  When healths and draughts go free—
Fishes that tipple in the deep
  Know no such liberty.

When, like committed linnets, I
    With shriller throat shall sing
The sweetness, mercy, majesty,
    And glories of my King;
When I shall voice aloud how good
    He is, how great should be,
Enlargèd winds, that curl the flood,
    Know no such liberty.

Stone walls do not a prison make,
    Nor iron bars a cage;
Minds innocent and quiet take
    That for an hermitage;
If I have freedom in my love
    And in my soul am free,
Angels alone, that soar above,
    Enjoy such liberty.

94

THE SICK ROSE

~

William Blake

A thousand interpreters have advanced a thousand interpretations of this small poem—evidence that Blake's genius discovered a set of universally potent symbols that work on a simple level of botany and zoology and on a higher level of Garden and Serpent, with many stops in between.

The conjunction of "joy" and "destroy" echoes Book IX of *Paradise Lost,* in which another flying invisible enemy invades a paradise. Milton's poem is mostly unrhymed, but "destroy" and "joy" end consecutive lines in one of Satan's soliloquies.

The Sick Rose

O Rose, thou art sick.
The invisible worm
That flies in the night
In the howling storm

Has found out thy bed
Of crimson joy,
And his dark secret love
Does thy life destroy.

95

ULYSSES

~

Alfred, Lord Tennyson

---

*T*hanks to James Joyce, Ezra Pound, and Nikos Kazantzakis, the character
known as Odysseus or Ulysses is the most durable legendary personage from
the myths of classical antiquity.

The character is of a type called the Trickster, so that Ulysses outwits
Polyphemus the Cyclops more by brains than by brawn; the Wooden Horse
that brought Troy down was Ulysses' idea. He was one of the Greek heroes
in Homer's *Iliad* and the single hero of Homer's *Odyssey*. Since Virgil's *Aeneid*
follows the structure of the *Odyssey,* we could regard Aeneas as an early var-
iation of the theme. By Dante's time, around 1300, Ulysses could be regarded
as a deceiver and blasphemer, so that Dante situates *his* Ulysses very far down
in Hell. Dante's Ulysses talks about a last trip, one after the ten-year home-
coming described by Homer—and it is this medieval vision of the hero that
seems to shape Tennyson's "Ulysses," which is a poem spoken as a dramatic
monologue by Ulysses addressing his mariners (already a departure from
Homer, who had Ulysses arrive home having lost all his company).

It we know Dante as well as Homer, we may be in some doubt as to the
exact sense of Tennyson's poem. It is, indeed, inspirational and stirring; its
attitude was likened to that of Cecil Rhodes and other architects of empire.
But, as we know, it is also a deceptive piece of rhetoric that leads to disaster;
besides, the vocabulary and rhythm of the conclusion, climaxing on "will" and
"not to yield," sounds like one of Satan's pep-rally orations in Milton's *Paradise
Lost.*

Ulysses

It little profits that an idle king,
By this still hearth, among these barren crags,
Matched with an agèd wife, I mete and dole
Unequal laws unto a savage race
That hoard, and sleep, and feed, and know not me.
I cannot rest from travel; I will drink
Life to the lees. All times I have enjoyed

Greatly, have suffered greatly, both with those
That loved me, and alone; on shore, and when
Through scudding drifts the rainy Hyades
Vexed the dim sea. I am become a name;
For always roaming with a hungry heart
Much have I seen and known—cities of men
And manners, climates, councils, governments,
Myself not least, but honored of them all—
And drunk delight of battle with my peers,
Far on the ringing plains of windy Troy.
I am a part of all that I have met;
Yet all experience is an arch wherethrough
Gleams that untraveled world whose margin fades
Forever and forever when I move.
How dull it is to pause, to make an end,
To rust unburnished, not to shine in use!
As though to breathe were life! Life piled on life
Were all too little, and of one to me
Little remains; but every hour is saved
From that eternal silence, something more,
A bringer of new things; and vile it were
For some three suns to store and hoard myself,
And this gray spirit yearning in desire
To follow knowledge like a sinking star,
Beyond the utmost bound of human thought.

   This is my son, mine own Telemachus,
To whom I leave the scepter and the isle—
Well-loved of me, discerning to fulfill
This labor, by slow prudence to make mild
A rugged people, and through soft degrees
Subdue them to the useful and the good.
Most blameless is he, centered in the sphere
Of common duties, decent not to fail
In offices of tenderness, and pay
Meet adoration to my household gods,
When I am gone. He works his work, I mine.

   There lies the port; the vessel puffs her sail; .
There gloom the dark, broad seas. My mariners,
Souls that have toiled, and wrought, and thought with me—
That ever with a frolic welcome took
The thunder and the sunshine, and opposed

Free hearts, free foreheads—you and I are old;
Old age hath yet his honor and his toil.
Death closes all; but something ere the end,
Some work of noble note, may yet be done,
Not unbecoming men that strove with Gods.
The lights begin to twinkle from the rocks;
The long day wanes, the low moon climbs; the deep
Moans round with many voices. Come, my friends,
'Tis not too late to seek a newer world.
Push off, and sitting well in order smite
The sounding furrows; for my purpose holds
To sail beyond the sunset, and the baths
Of all the western stars, until I die.
It may be that the gulfs will wash us down;
It may be we shall touch the Happy Isles,
And see the great Achilles, whom we knew.
Though much is taken, much abides; and though
We are not now that strength which in old days
Moved earth and heaven, that which we are, we are—
One equal temper of heroic hearts,
Made weak by time and fate, but strong in will
To strive, to seek, to find, and not to yield.

96

THE EAGLE

~

Alfred, Lord Tennyson

A brief and flawless heraldic realization of a creature in all the spikily tangible properties of his creatureliness.

The Eagle

He clasps the crag with crooked hands;
Close to the sun in lonely lands,
Ringed with the azure world, he stands.

The wrinkled sea beneath him crawls;
He watches from his mountain walls,
And like a thunderbolt he falls.

97

HOME-THOUGHTS, FROM ABROAD

~

Robert Browning

---

*B*rowning published this poem and a companion-piece, "Home-Thoughts, from the Sea," in 1845, both imagined from the viewpoint of an Englishman in or near the southwest corner of the Continent. Even the wording of "Home-Thoughts" is peculiarly English (or Germanic, at any rate), different from a corresponding expression in French or Italian.

Presumably, you never appreciate what you have at home until you spend some time away. The English may feel indifference or contempt toward the climate, fauna, and flora of their home island in the ironically named Temperate Zone. But their minds are changed by too-long residence in equatorial, tropical, or subtropical climes where birds and flowers and music can all be too loud, too gaudy.

Home-Thoughts, from Abroad

I

Oh, to be in England
Now that April's there,
And whoever wakes in England
Sees, some morning, unaware,
That the lowest boughs and the brushwood sheaf
Round the elm-tree bole are in tiny leaf,
While the chaffinch sings on the orchard bough
In England—now!

II

And after April, when May follows,
And the whitethroat builds, and all the swallows!
Hark, where my blossomed pear tree in the hedge
Leans to the field and scatters on the clover
Blossoms and dewdrops—at the bent spray's edge—
That's the wise thrush; he sings each song twice over,

Lest you should think he never could recapture
The first fine careless rapture!
And though the fields look rough with hoary dew,
All will be gay when noontide wakes anew
The buttercups, the little children's dower
—Far brighter than this gaudy melon-flower!

98

A NARROW FELLOW IN THE GRASS

~

Emily Dickinson

*C*harms and riddles are among the oldest of poems, and they are also, in a sense, the "oldest" or earliest poems for most readers. The point normally is to describe something without naming it. There are riddles in the Bible, in Homer, in Old English literature (not all solved, either), and in any schoolyard or workplace.

Intrusive annotation is like a bad-breathed usher who takes you to your seat and then stays alongside you and explains everything. Most people prefer to figure things out for themselves; that is why I have kept explanations and interpretations to a minimum. I certainly shall not give away this riddle.

A Narrow Fellow in the Grass

A narrow Fellow in the Grass
Occasionally rides—
You may have met Him—did you not
His notice sudden is—

The Grass divides as with a Comb—
A spotted shaft is seen—
And then it closes at your feet
And opens further on—

He likes a Boggy Acre
A Floor too cool for Corn—
Yet when a Boy, and Barefoot—
I more than once at Noon
Have passed, I thought, a Whip lash
Unbraiding in the Sun
When stooping to secure it
It wrinkled, and was gone—

Several of Nature's People
I know, and they know me—
I feel for them a transport
Of cordiality—

But never met this Fellow
Attended, or alone
Without a tighter breathing
And Zero at the Bone—

99

WHEN YOU ARE OLD

~

William Butler Yeats

Yeats wrote few translations, and in fact there are not many translations or adaptations (maybe a better term for what Yeats did) in this book, so "When You Are Old," against the odds, represents a reworking by the young Yeats (in 1892) of a poem by the sixteenth-century French poet Pierre Ronsard, "Quand vous serez bien vielle, au soir à la chandelle."

When You Are Old

When you are old and gray and full of sleep,
And nodding by the fire, take down this book,
And slowly read, and dream of the soft look
Your eyes had once, and of their shadows deep;

How many loved your moments of glad grace,
And loved your beauty with love false or true,
But one man loved the pilgrim soul in you,
And loved the sorrows of your changing face;

And bending down beside the glowing bars,
Murmur, a little sadly, how love fled
And paced upon the mountains overhead
And hid his face amid a crowd of stars.

THE LISTENERS

~

Walter De La Mare

---

*A*s a young man in London, Walter de la Mare was a bookkeeper for the Anglo-American Oil Company. Such commercial experience links him to Wallace Stevens, Franz Kafka, and Charles Ives, all of whom had some connection with the insurance business. Such a destiny may seem horrible to the literary and academic audience for poetry—and it may have *been* horrible to those who underwent it—but there is at least a chance that some steady employment in a no-nonsense business that attends to the real world in a hard-headed practical way does two things for an artist: provides a regular income and releases the imagination. If one's daily work gets rid of the drive to be practical and realistic, then one's leisure can be devoted to the fanciful, the fabulous, the idealistic, and the experimental.

With de la Mare, the world of poetry is a shadowland between childhood and adulthood, dream and waking; the details and significances may remain somewhat vague, but the vigorous presentation makes the work—however elliptical or parabolic (and "The Listeners" sounds like a parable)—most effective.

Thomas Hardy, according to his widow's account of his last days, at the end "could no longer listen to the reading of prose, though a short poem now and again interested him. In the middle of one night he asked his wife to read aloud to him 'The Listeners,' by Walter de la Mare."

The Listeners

"Is there anybody there?" said the Traveler,
    Knocking on the moonlit door;
And his horse in the silence champed the grasses
    Of the forest's ferny floor:
And a bird flew up out of the turret,
    Above the Traveler's head:
And he smote upon the door again a second time;
    "Is there anybody there?" he said.
But no one descended to the Traveler;
    No head from the leaf-fringed sill

Leaned over and looked into his gray eyes,
    Where he stood perplexed and still.
But only a host of phantom listeners
    That dwelt in the lone house then
Stood listening in the quiet of the moonlight
    To that voice from the world of men:
Stood thronging the faint moonbeams on the dark stair,
    That goes down to the empty hall,
Hearkening in an air stirred and shaken
    By the lonely Traveler's call.
And he felt in his heart their strangeness,
    Their stillness answering his cry,
While his horse moved, cropping the dark turf,
    'Neath the starred and leafy sky;
For he suddenly smote on the door, even
    Louder, and lifted his head: —
"Tell them I came, and no one answered,
    That I kept my word," he said.
Never the least stir made the listeners,
    Though every word he spake
Fell echoing through the shadowiness of the still house
    From the one man left awake:
Ay, they heard his foot upon the stirrup,
    And the sound of iron on stone,
And how the silence surged softly backward,
    When the plunging hoofs were gone.

NOTES ON THE POEMS

POEM 2, ANONYMOUS, "SIR PATRICK SPENS"

skeely skillful
lift sky
lap sprang
laith unwilling
aboon above
flatter'd floated, tossing
kames combs

POEM 3, JOHN KEATS, "TO AUTUMN"

hook scythe
sallows willows
bourn region
croft a small enclosed field

POEM 4, WILLIAM SHAKESPEARE, "THAT TIME OF YEAR THOU MAYST IN ME BEHOLD"

or none, or few either none or few

POEM 5, GERARD MANLEY HOPKINS, "PIED BEAUTY"

The poem is in a form devised by Hopkins, the "Curtal Sonnet," which preserves the 4:3 ratio of the octave and sestet of the italian sonnet but reduces the first section to six lines. since 4:3::6:4.5, the second section has only four and a fraction lines.

brinded brindled
stipple dots
trim equipment
counter contrary, with opposing patterns

POEM 7, SAMUEL TAYLOR COLERIDGE, "KUBLA KHAN"

Here are the first two paragraphs of coleridge's celebrated introduction to the poem:

The following fragment is here published at the request of a poet of great and deserved celebrity, and, as far as the author's own opinions are concerned, rather a psychological curiosity, than on the ground of any supposed *poetic* merits.

In the summer of the year 1797, the author, then in ill health, had retired to a lonely farmhouse between Porlock and Linton, on the Exmoor confines of Somerset and Devonshire. In consequence of a slight indisposition, an anodyne had been prescribed, from the effects of which he fell asleep in his chair at the moment that he was reading the following sentence, or words of the same substance, in *Purchas's Pilgrimage:* "Here the Kubla Khan commanded a palace to be built, and a stately garden thereunto. And thus ten miles of fertile ground were inclosed with a wall." The author continued for about three hours in a profound sleep, at least of the external senses, during which time he has the most vivid confidence that he could not have composed less than from two to three hundred lines; if that indeed can be called composition in which all the images rose up before him as *things,* with a parallel production of the correspondent expressions, without any sensation or consciousness of effort. on awaking he appeared to himself to have a distinct recollection of the whole, and taking his pen, ink, and paper, instantly and eagerly wrote down the lines that are here preserved. At this moment he was unfortunately called out by a person on business from Porlock, and detained by him above an hour, and on his return to his room, found, to his no small surprise and mortification, that though he still retained some vague and dim recollection of the general purport of the vision, yet, with the exception of some eight or ten scattered lines and images, all the rest had passed away like the images on the surface of a stream into which a stone has been cast, but, alas! without the after restoration of the latter!

POEM 8, MATTHEW ARNOLD, "DOVER BEACH"

shingles   pebbled beaches

POEM 9, JOHN KEATS, "LA BELLE DAME SANS MERCI"

Zone   girdle
latest   last

POEM 11, ANDREW MARVELL, "TO HIS COY MISTRESS"

Humber   estuary in Marvell's native region in northeast England, formed by the Ouse and Trent Rivers
vegetable   not so much in the sense of "plantlike" as in the sense, supported by etymology, of "living, lively, capable of growth"

POEM 12, CHRISTOPHER MARLOWE, "THE PASSIONATE SHEPHERD TO HIS LOVE"

prove   test, try, probe

POEM 13, JOHN DONNE, "DEATH, BE NOT PROUD"

delivery   deliverance, liberty
poppy   opium

POEM 14, ROBERT HERRICK, "UPON JULIA'S CLOTHES"

brave   splendid

POEM 16, WILLIAM WORDSWORTH, "THE WORLD IS TOO MUCH WITH US"

boon   gift

POEM 17, JOHN KEATS, "ON FIRST LOOKING INTO CHAPMAN'S HOMER"

demesne   domain, realm
Darien   in Panama

POEM 18, LEWIS CARROLL, "JABBERWOCKY"

Humpty Dumpty explains some of the words to Alice in *Through the Looking-Glass:*
brillig   "four o'clock in the afternoon—the time when you begin *broiling* things for dinner"
slithy   "slimy" plus "lithe"
toves   "something like badgers . . . something like lizards . . . something like corkscrews"
gyre and gimble   "to go round and round like a gyroscope" and "to make holes like a gimlet"
wabe   "the grass plot around a sundial"
mimsy   "flimsy" plus "miserable"
borogove   "a thin shabby-looking bird with its feathers sticking out all round—something like a live mop"
mome   possibly "from home"
rath   "a sort of green pig"
outgrabe   something between "whistle" and "bellow" (with overtones from German *Grabe*, "grave")

POEM 19, WILLIAM BUTLER YEATS, "THE SECOND COMING"

Spiritus Mundi   the spirit of the world, soul of the universe, the Great Memory containing all the true images of the species

POEM 20, THOMAS GRAY, "ELEGY WRITTEN IN A COUNTRY CHURCHYARD"

rude   rustic
echoing horn   in hunting
glebe   soil
fretted   ornamented
animated   lifelike
provoke   summon
Hampden   opposed Charles I, killed in the Civil Wars
madding   milling
Science   Learning or Knowledge in general

POEM 21, PERCY BYSSHE SHELLEY, "OZYMANDIAS"

hand that mocked them   the sculptor's, "mocked" meaning both "imitated" and "ridiculed"
heart   the king's

POEM 22, WILLIAM BUTLER YEATS, "SAILING TO BYZANTIUM"

perne   spin

POEM 23, WILLIAM SHAKESPEARE, "SHALL I COMPARE THEE TO A SUMMER'S DAY?"

untrimm'd   stripped
ow'st   ownest

POEM 24, WILLIAM SHAKESPEARE, "LET ME NOT TO THE MARRIAGE OF TRUE MINDS"

height   probably the altitude of the star, its angular height above the horizon, measured in degrees; possibly the height of the masthead of the bark as well, a trigonometric calculation that could suggest the weight of the vessel but not necessarily the worth of ship or cargo

POEM 25, WILLIAM SHAKESPEARE, "FEAR NO MORE THE HEAT O' THE SUN"

thunder stone   meteorite (thought to be the cause of thunder)

POEM 26, JOHN KEATS, "ODE TO A NIGHTINGALE"

hemlock   poison from the leaves of the European plant of the parsley family (*Conium macalatum*)
Lethe   the river in hell that brings forgetfulness
Flora   Roman goddess of flowers
Hippocrene   fountain of the Muses on Mount Helicon
pards   leopards
Fays   fairies
embalmed   perfumed
eglantine   European rose; sweetbrier
corn   wheat

POEM 27, T. S. ELIOT, "THE LOVE SONG OF J. ALFRED PRUFROCK"

S'io credessi   The epigraph, from Dante, *Inferno* XXVII, is spoken by the deceptive Guido da Montefeltro: "If I could believe that my response were being made to a person who might return to the world above, this flame would be still without further movement; but, since no one has ever gone back alive from this depth—if I hear the truth—I shall respond to you without fear of infamy."
magic lantern   an old-fashioned slide projector

POEM 28, EDGAR ALLAN POE, "TO HELEN"

Nicéan   never precisely elucidated; perhaps related to Nicaea or Nice
Naiad   having to do with the nymphs associated with springs, fountains, rivers, and lakes

POEM 29, EMILY DICKINSON, "BECAUSE I COULD NOT STOP FOR DEATH"

Gossamer   thin, filmy cloth
Tippet   the hanging part of a hood or cape
Tulle   fine netting of silk

POEM 30, GERARD MANLEY HOPKINS, "THE WINDHOVER"

dauphin   prince, heir
wimpling   bending, like the wimples that are part of the habits of certain nuns
Buckle   come together as well as fall apart

sillion   ridge between furrows

Fall, gall, etc.   The imagery and color scheme here suggest both the Crucifixion and the Eucharist.

POEM 31, WILFRED OWEN, "ANTHEM FOR DOOMED YOUTH"

orisons   prayers
pall   a piece of cloth—probably white in this context, to answer to "pallor" earlier—covering a coffin

POEM 32, WILLIAM SHAKESPEARE, "WHEN ICICLES HANG BY THE WALL"

keel   stir
saw   wise saying; also, drone
crabs   crab apples

POEM 33, JOHN DONNE, "BATTER MY HEART, THREE-PERSONED GOD"

captived   held captive

POEM 35, PERCY BYSSHE SHELLEY, "ODE TO THE WEST WIND"

Maenad   frenzied female adherent of Dionysus
Baiae's bay   near Naples
lyre   the Eolian lyre (or harp), which was played by the wind

POEM 36, GERARD MANLEY HOPKINS, "GOD'S GRANDEUR"

The end of the poem seems a study in the Welsh device called "cynghanedd," which is multiple alliteration in patterns of either *xyxy* (alternating) or *xyyx* (chiastic). both appear at the end:

> World *br*oods with *w*arm *br*east and with ah! *br*ight *w*ings.

oil   from olives

POEM 37, DYLAN THOMAS, "DO NOT GO GENTLE INTO THAT GOOD NIGHT"

The alternating alliteration in the sequence of adjectives "wise . . . Good . . . Wild . . . Grave" illustrates an ancient Welsh device called "cynghanedd," also present in "God's Grandeur" and other poems by Gerard Manley Hopkins.

POEM 39, SIR THOMAS WYATT, "THE LOVER SHOWETH HOW HE IS FORSAKEN OF SUCH AS HE SOMETIME ENJOYED"

small slender
kindly after the fashion of her kind (womankind), with play on meanings of "kindness" and "kindliness"
fain eagerly, gladly

POEM 40, JOHN DONNE, "THE GOOD-MORROW"

the seven sleepers' den the cave in which seven youths of Ephesus took refuge to escape persecution; they slept for nearly 200 years
Let maps to others, worlds on worlds have shown Let it be that maps have shown worlds on worlds to others

POEM 41, ROBERT HERRICK, "DELIGHT IN DISORDER"

stomacher an ornamented triangular piece of cloth covering the chest and abdomen

POEM 43, ROBERT BROWNING, "MY LAST DUCHESS"

Frà Pandolph, Claus of Innsbruck not actual artists
favor present

POEM 44, GERARD MANLEY HOPKINS, "SPRING AND FALL"

leafmeal leaf-by-leaf (by analogy with "piecemeal") and ground into a meal
ghost soul or spirit (as in Holy Ghost)

POEM 46, EZRA POUND, "THE RIVER-MERCHANT'S WIFE: A LETTER"

A free translation of "The Song of Ch'ang-Kan" by Li Po (called "Rihaku" in Japanese).
My Lord you presumably a highly formal second-person pronoun
river Kiang "Kiang" actually means "river"; the original has "the Three Gorges"
Cho-fu-Sa literally, "Long Wind Sand" (*fu* = "wind," as in *typhoon*)

POEM 47, EDMUND WALLER, "GO, LOVELY ROSE"

resemble liken

POEM 48, HENRY VAUGHAN, "THE RETREAT"

sev'ral separate

POEM 49, JOHN KEATS, "ODE ON A GRECIAN URN"

Sylvan of the woods; rustic
Tempe, Arcady regions of ancient Greece, associated with pastoral beauty
Attic relating to Attica, the region of ancient Greece that included Athens
brede braided pattern
overwrought ornamented all over

POEM 50, WILLIAM BLAKE, "LONDON"

charter'd given a charter of liberty, but also marked out as property
plagues venereal disease
hearse a bier, here involving combination with marriage bed

POEM 51, WILLIAM BLAKE, "AND DID THOSE FEET"

those feet Christ's
Mills machinery in both the general sense (as a grain mill) and the more recent industrial sense, probably with smoke-producing fuel

POEM 54, THOMAS HARDY, "THE DARKLING THRUSH"

coppice a copse or stand of hardwood trees left standing to be cut down (*coupée*) later; usually fenced and gated

POEM 57, DYLAN THOMAS, "FERN HILL"

dingle small, deep, wooded valley

POEM 58, THOMAS NASHE, "A LITANY IN TIME OF PLAGUE"

Fond foolish
toys trifles
Physic himself medical science itself

POEM 59, BEN JONSON, "SONG: TO CELIA"

change here seems to mean "accept in exchange for"

POEM 60, GEORGE HERBERT, "THE COLLAR"

board table
cordial life-giving

POEM 61, SIR JOHN SUCKLING, "WHY SO PALE AND WAN, FOND LOVER?"

Prithee I pray thee
this will not move this will not move her

POEM 62, ANDREW MARVELL, "THE GARDEN"

palm, oak, bays customarily awarded for accomplishment in athletics, civic affairs, and poetry
sacred plants cuttings
all but rude "all nothing but rude"
vest clothing
dial evidently a sundial made of flowers

POEM 65, ALFRED, LORD TENNYSON, "CROSSING THE BAR"

bar a sandbar formed along an ocean beach, crossable only at high tide ("Too full for sound and foam")

POEM 66, EDWIN ARLINGTON ROBINSON, "MR. FLOOD'S PARTY"

the poet says in Edward FitzGerald's translation of *The Rubáiyát of Omar Khayyám*
Roland's ghost Charlemagne's noblest knight guarded the pass at Roncevaux, refusing to blow his horn for help until it was too late

POEM 67, W. H. AUDEN, "MUSÉE DES BEAUX ARTS"

Title: Museum of Fine Arts—close to the name of the museum in Brussels that houses many Brueghel paintings
Icarus The painting is variously titled "The Fall of Icarus" and "Landscape with the Fall of Icarus," the latter emphasizing the thematic design discussed in the poem.

POEM 70, WILLIAM SHAKESPEARE, "WHEN TO THE SESSIONS OF SWEET SILENT THOUGHT"

sessions the sitting of a court
wail bewail
dateless endless
tell count (as a bank *teller* does)

POEM 74, EDWIN ARLINGTON ROBINSON, "MINIVER CHEEVY"

Thebes name of ancient Egyptian and Greek cities, the latter associated with Oedipus and his offspring, including the two sons whose rivalry instigated the Seven Against Thebes
Camelot legendary seat of Arthur's kingdom
Priam king of Troy at time of the Trojan War
Medici illustrious, if cruel, family of Italian Renaissance merchant-princes; ruled Florence for decades and generously supported artists

POEM 75, HART CRANE, "TO BROOKLYN BRIDGE"

guerdon reward

POEM 76, ANONYMOUS, "EDWARD, EDWARD"

brand sword
dree suffer
bairns children

POEM 79, BEN JONSON, "ON MY FIRST SON"

lose all father give up all thoughts of fatherhood

POEM 80, JOHN DONNE, "AT THE ROUND EARTH'S IMAGINED CORNERS"

never taste death's woe Matthew XVI:28 and two other places in the Gospels record that Christ promised that some "will not taste death before they see the Son of man coming in his kingdom."

POEM 84, GEORGE HERBERT, "VIRTUE"

sweets perfumes
closes in music, a concluding cadence

POEM 82, THOMAS CAREW, "ASK ME NO MORE WHERE JOVE BESTOWS"

sphere the fixed stars were thought to be embedded in their own celestial sphere
phoenix a mythological bird that burns up and is reborn from its own ashes every 500 years

POEM 83, THOMAS GRAY, "ODE ON THE DEATH OF A FAVORITE CAT, DROWNED IN A TUB OF GOLD FISHES"

blow   bloom
Genii   guardian spirits
Tyrian   purple
Nereid   sea-nymph

POEM 84, SAMUEL TAYLOR COLERIDGE, "THE RIME OF THE ANCIENT MARINER"

Facile credo, etc. Adapted by Coleridge from Thomas Burnet's *Archaeologiae Philosophicae* (1692): "I can easily believe that there are more invisible than visible beings in the universe. But of their families, degrees, connections, distinctions, and functions, who shall tell us? How do they act? Where are they found? About such matters the human mind has always circled without attaining knowledge. Yet I do not doubt that sometimes it is well for the soul to contemplate as in a picture the image of a larger and better world, lest the mind, habituated to the small concerns of daily life, limit itself too much and sink entirely into trivial thinking. But meanwhile we must be on watch for the truth, avoiding extremes, so that we may distinguish certain from uncertain, day from night."

Part I
Eftsoons   straightway
kirk   church
clifts   cliffs
swound   swoon
Part II
uprist   arose
Part III
wist   knew
Gramercy   great thanks! Thank heaven!
weal   benefit
Part IV
hoary   gray
Part V
silly   harmless
sheen   shone
corses   corpses
jargoning   warbling
I have not to declare   I cannot declare
Part VI
rood   cross
seraph-man   angel-like
shrieve   free from sin
Part VII
tod   clump
crossed his brow   made the sign of the Cross
forlorn   deprived

POEM 85, RALPH WALDO EMERSON, "CONCORD HYMN"

Monument commemorating the battles of Lexington and Concord, April 19, 1775

POEM 86, WILLIAM BUTLER YEATS, "THE LAKE ISLE OF INNISFREE"

wattles sticks, stakes, twigs, and branches intertwined

POEM 89, SIR WALTER RALEGH, "THE NYMPH'S REPLY TO THE SHEPHERD"

Philomel the nightingale
kirtle long dress
date time of ending

POEM 90, JOHN DONNE, "GO AND CATCH A FALLING STAR"

mandrake poisonous plant of the nightshade family (*Mandragora offinarum*) with a thick, forked root
mermaids women, like the Sirens and the Lorelei, whose beautiful singing lures sailors to their death; also, "to hear mermaids singing" symbolizes the coming of death

POEM 91, JOHN DONNE, "THE SUN RISING"

offices chores
spice and mine the East and West Indias, or Indies, associated with spices and gold mines, respectively
alchemy here, an example of the bogus
center center of the sun's orbit

POEM 92, JOHN MILTON, "LYCIDAS"

Monody dirge for single voice
laurels, myrtles, ivy associated with Apollo (poetry), Venus (love), and Bacchus (revelry)
crude unripe
dear deeply moving
meed reward
lawns pastures
oaten flute panpipes
canker cankerworm
blows blossoms
Mona Anglesey
Deva the Dee
the Muse herself that Orpheus bore Calliope

gory visage   the head of Orpheus floated down the Hebrus River and out into the Aegean to Lesbos
boots   profits
guerdon   reward
the blind Fury   Atropos
Phoebus   Apollo
Arethuse   Arethusa, a fountain in Sicily, associated with Theocritus
Mincius   river in Lombardy, associated with Virgil
the herald of the sea   Triton
Hippotades   the god of the winds, Aeolus, who was the son of Hippotas ·
Panope   the chief sea nymph
Camus   supposed god of the River Cam
pilot   St. Peter
Two massy keys   perhaps keys to open and to shut the gates of heaven
list   choose, like
scrannel   harsh, meager
the grim wolf   Roman Catholicism
that two-handed engine   meaning uncertain
swart star   Sirius, the dog star
rathe   early, eager
freak'd   freckled
hearse   bier
Bellerus   fabled giant, buried in Cornwall
Namancos, Bayona   in Spain
ruth   pity
tricks   dresses
unexpressive nuptial song   inexpressible hymn of joy
genius   spirit
uncouth swain   supposedly unlearned shepherd
Doric   rustic
Thus sang, etc.   The final eight lines follow the rhyme scheme of the stanza called ottava rima (*ababababcc*)

POEM 93, RICHARD LOVELACE, "TO ALTHEA, FROM PRISON"

committed linnets   caged songbirds

POEM 95, ALFRED, LORD TENNYSON, "ULYSSES"

Hyades   a group of 200 stars in the constellation Taurus, associated with rainy weather
the Happy Isles   the abode of the favored dead

POEM 98, EMILY DICKINSON, "A NARROW FELLOW IN THE GRASS"

This poem displays a number of unique technical features, appropriate in a charm of riddle. The consonant pattern of the line "His notice sudden is" is virtually a mirror image (z-n-t-s-s-d-n-z). Throughout, all the rhymes are somehow deficient until the very last: "alone" and "bone" constitute the only perfect rhyme in the poem.

BIOGRAPHIES OF THE POETS

MATTHEW ARNOLD, 1822–1888

Matthew Arnold was the son of the famous Dr. Thomas Arnold, headmaster of Rugby and, toward the end of his life in 1842, Professor of Modern History at Oxford. Like another father-and-son team—James and John Stuart Mill—Thomas and Matthew Arnold exerted a potent influence over English cultural life for much of the nineteenth century. In 1851 Matthew Arnold was appointed an inspector of schools; six years later he was named to the Chair of Poetry at Oxford, holding the appointment for ten years. In addition to his poetry, he produced a substantial amount of important aesthetic and cultural criticism.

W. H. AUDEN, 1907–1973

Gertrude Stein, Ezra Pound, and T. S. Eliot, among many others, were American-born writers who emigrated to Europe and spent much of their adult lives in exile. Wystan Hugh Auden, with characteristic audacity, reversed the trend. Even after spectacular success as the leader of a generation who emerged strongly and brilliantly in England in the 1930s, Auden moved to the United States in 1939 and became a citizen in 1946. Only at the very end of his life did he move back to England. He was thoroughly modern. Born in the twentieth century, he was at home with science, technology, and engineering; his father was a physician, and Auden claimed to have entertained child-hood ambitions of becoming a mining engineer. Auden also took to modernist psy-chology (represented by Freud and by Homer Lane as well) and modernist economics (represented by Marx). Auden was a chameleon of styles and tones, and he probably commanded a greater range of forms and idioms than any other twentieth-century poet. He was also a notable essayist, critic, teacher, and editor.

WILLIAM BLAKE, 1757–1827

A Londoner, Blake was a poet, painter, engraver, and visionary. *Songs of Innocence* and *Songs of Experience,* words and designs alike, were engraved on copper by Blake himself. After an early period of relatively simple lyrics, Blake turned to the production of visionary poems of great originality and scope; his last works were *Jerusalem* and *Milton.* Blake's unique combination of sophistication, naivete, sublimity, piety, and coarseness impresses many as peculiarly English; his influence continues today among painters and writers on both sides of the Atlantic, and there is something that can be called authentically Blakean in the poetry of the American Allen Ginsberg as well as in the prose of the Irishman Joyce Cary (especially the character Gulley Jimson in *The Horse's Mouth* and other novels).

ROBERT BROWNING, 1812–1889

The most sensational episode in Robert Browning's life was his elopement with Elizabeth Barrett, a piece of history made perhaps all too familiar in the popular play called *The Barretts of Wimpole Street.* Even so, they were in love, and they did escape to Italy, and a little bit of romantic adventure, even if exaggerated, won't do any harm. As an adolescent and young man, Browning experimented with a great variety of types of poetry, but his twentieth-century reputation owes most to his perfection of the so-called dramatic monologue. Some of these poems are more properly classified as soliloquies or epistles, but the fundamental idea is the same: one person utters a single sustained expression under some pressure that causes a revelation of character. Since the regulations limit such poetry, Browning did not often invent characters from scratch. Instead, he took existing literary characters (such as Caliban from Shakespeare's *The Tempest*), real historical characters (such as Fra Lippo Lippi and Andrea del Sarto), or familiar types (such as Renaissance Italian dukes and bishops). The Brownings, both of whom were notable poets, lived in Florence from 1846 until her death in 1861. Robert Browning then returned to England, where he was to spend most of his remaining days. He died in Venice, but the body was brought back to England and buried with honor in Westminster Abbey.

GEORGE GORDON NOEL BYRON, 6TH BARON BYRON 1788–1824

Even among the stellar company of these great poets, Lord Byron stands out as uniquely distinguished—maybe more for his personality and life than for his poetry as such, although he is widely regarded as a very great poet indeed, especially as a wit and satirist. Byron was not only a genius, he was also a millionaire, a hero, a nobleman, a sinner, and a beauty. The world is still learning how to catch up with him. He was born into a tormented and tempestuous family; his father, who died when Byron was three, was nicknamed "Mad Jack." Byron succeeded to the family title when he was ten; his schooling was at Harrow and Cambridge. He began publishing poetry while still in his teens, and by 1812 was among the most famous poets in England. He married most unhappily in 1815, and in the next year—hounded by accusations of insanity and incest—he exiled himself, never to come home. In addition to a number of excellent short lyrics, Byron is remembered today for his two most ambitious poems, *Childe Harold's Pilgrimage* and *Don Juan*. There have been better poets, but none has surpassed Byron in personal influence: the "Byronic hero" is still with us—dark, moody, aloof, misanthropic, courageous, brilliant, tortured.

THOMAS CAREW, 1595–1639

Carew, a lawyer's son, was educated in the law at Oxford and the Middle Temple. He is included among the "Courtly" poets who specialized in lighthearted (but not lightheaded) lyrics in praise of love.

"LEWIS CARROLL" (CHARLES LUTWIDGE DODGSON) 1832–1898

To form his celebrated pseudonym, Dodgson dropped his last name, reversed the order of his first two names, and converted them from rather dense Northern forms to something more Latinate. He also transformed his complex personality, or personalities. He was an ordained minister and also an accomplished mathematician and classicist, but a deeper self communicated with children, mostly little girls. To amuse Alice Liddell, he wrote something first called "Alice's Adventures Underground," eventually published as *Alice's Adventures in Wonderland* (1865), followed by *Through the Looking-Glass and What Alice Found There* (1871). As if all these achievements were not enough, Dodgson was also a very fine photographer.

SAMUEL TAYLOR COLERIDGE, 1772–1834

Coleridge belongs in the company of the great collaborators, the great poet-critics, and—paradoxically—the great popular poets. The paradox is that the most philosophical of philosophical critics, fit for the company of Plato and Bacon, should also be the least philosophical of poets, fit for the company of the anonymous authors of "Sir Patrick Spens" and "Edward, Edward." The son of a vicar, Coleridge received a spotty but stimulating education and led a peculiarly vexed life, which included a dependency on opium. He was, however, most fortunate in his associations; he was close to Charles Lamb, William Wordsworth, and Robert Southey, and he was supported for several years by the philanthropy of Josiah and Thomas Wedgwood, still famous for their china.

HART CRANE, 1899–1932

Around the end of the nineteenth century, the American Midwest produced a group of varied and impressive writers who sought to distil the essential meanings of individual life and of American experience in general: F. Scott Fitzgerald, Ernest Hemingway (born on the same day as Hart Crane), and (Harold) Hart Crane of Ohio, who, in a tragically short and sad life, became one of America's most ambitious and most eloquent poets. Crane's father was a candy manufacturer whose marriage to a complex, cultivated woman was turbulent and finally dissolved. Crane was tormented all his life by difficult relations—with both parents, with friends, and with lovers, male and female. But, through all the troubles, Crane sought to perfect his great gifts of vision and expression. He never even finished high school but sought instead to educate himself by reading and by living. He spent significant portions of his life in New York, Florida, the Caribbean, and Mexico. It was on a return journey from Mexico that he jumped from a ship, evidently (though not certainly) a suicide.

WALTER DE LA MARE, 1873–1956

Walter de la Mare, who was born in Kent, was too poor to go to school beyond adolescence. He worked for many years as a bookkeeper for a petroleum conglomerate, and it was not until he was in middle age that he was free to spend all his time as a writer. He was best known for his poetry, but he also wrote fiction, including the celebrated *Memoirs of a Midget* (1931). De la Mare's poetry was prized and praised by Thomas Hardy, T. S. Eliot, and W. H. Auden.

EMILY DICKINSON, 1830–1886

Dickinson was born in Amherst, Massachusetts, and spent most of her strange life there. She was the daughter of a lawyer who served in the United States House of Representatives. She seems to have been an outgoing and gregarious young woman but became more reclusive as years passed. Of her many poems—upwards of 1800—only seven or eight were published in her lifetime. In this respect she resembles Gerard Manley Hopkins. Since she was such a great and eloquent poet, people have naturally been interested in finding out more about her; but biographical speculations have run into many barriers, and her poetry itself continues to present enigmas, anomalies, and opacities still. Whatever the truth about her life, she remains a poet of unmatched strength and vitality, and the primitive simplicity of some of her stanzas is balanced by the audacious complexity of some of her rhymes and rhythms. In some ways it is just impossible to imagine Emily Dickinson flourishing anywhere but the United States in the middle of the nineteenth century. Early collections of her poems were heavily— maybe impudently—edited with a lot of normalization and sanitizing; heroic work by Thomas Johnson from 1955 onwards did something to establish a text more like what Dickinson actually wrote, with many peculiarities of punctuation.

JOHN DONNE, 1572–1631

Donne began as a Roman Catholic but later, while studying law, joined the Church of England. He was a traveler, diplomat, and courtier. Rather late in life, he became a preacher, and was soon famous for his sermons; he was made Dean of St. Paul's in 1621. As the poems in this book demonstrate, Donne could write, with equal facility and depth, passionate poems of secular love and passionate poems of sacred love, both sorts informed by large-minded wit.

ERNEST DOWSON, 1867–1900

Although Dowson was born in Kent and schooled at Oxford, he spent much of his short life in France, the incarnation of dissipation and decadence. He was consumptive and made his condition worse by drinking. While living in the slummy East End of London, he met his "Cynara," a café-owner's daughter who was to marry a waiter.

MICHAEL DRAYTON, 1563–1631

Drayton, who came from Warwickshire, like Shakespeare, was a Jack of all poetic genres, excelling in the sonnet (such as the poem in this book) and also in historical and topographical poems; moreover, he collaborated on various dramatic works. He was among the earliest of the professional men of letters and is buried, deservedly, in Westminster Abbey.

T. S. ELIOT, 1888–1965

Thomas Stearns Eliot was born in St. Louis, Missouri, on the banks of the Mississippi River, and later spoke of his background as, variously, Southwestern or Midwestern (not very precise terms); even so, his deeper loyalty seems to have been to New England, where he was a Harvard student and where his family had a summer home, and later to Old England, to which he emigrated in 1914 and where he stayed, becoming a British subject in 1927. His education was more in philosophy than in literature, and he all-but-finished the work for a doctorate at Harvard. He worked as an officer of Lloyds Bank for quite a few years, and then became a valued member of the directorate of the publishing firm Faber and Faber. During the 1920s he established a potent reputation as a poet and as a critic, also editing the influential magazine *The Criterion* (1922–39). Like Thomas Hardy, he was given the rare and coveted Order of Merit; like W. B. Yeats, he was awarded the Nobel Prize for Literature—the only American-born poet to be so honored.

RALPH WALDO EMERSON, 1803–1882

Emerson was born in Boston and spent most of his life there and at two other nearby Massachusetts towns, Cambridge and Concord. His early training was that of a school-master and Unitarian pastor, but from about his thirtieth year he earned his living as an essayist and lecturer. His poetry is respected, but his fame rests much more on his distinctly American labors as a philosopher and thinker. He made three trips to Europe and was friendly with Thomas Carlyle and other European eminences. He kept up with affairs and trends in the United States and in Europe, and it is to his credit that he was among the first to recognize the genius of Walt Whitman.

ROBERT FROST, 1874–1963

It is anomalous (but maybe peculiarly American) that Frost should be so strongly associated with the idiom and landscape of New England, since he was born in California (west of the Mississippi River, like the birthplaces of Ezra Pound, Marianne Moore, and T. S. Eliot) and named for Robert E. Lee, the great Confederate general. But Frost was raised a New Englander and the titles of many of his books insist on the identification: *North of Boston* obviously, *A Boy's Will* more subtly (the phrase comes from a poem by Longfellow, who was born in Maine), *New Hampshire* undeniably. Frost lived mostly in New Hampshire and Vermont but also spent significant periods in Michigan and Florida. He was unique in his power to combine a modernist sensibility and learning with a knack for the truly popular. In "Mending Wall" he became the only modern poet who could genuinely be said to have written a proverb: "Good fences make good neighbors."

THOMAS GRAY, 1716–1771

Like John Milton, Thomas Gray was the son of a scrivener. Gray was born in London and educated at Eton and Cambridge. Although he had a law degree, he never practiced, choosing instead to devote his life to the study of language, literature, and antiquities. Toward the end of his life he was awarded the Professorship of Modern History at Cambridge. Gray was a wonderfully versatile poet, and, though he may not rank among the top superstars, his "Elegy" is probably better known than poems by more celebrated figures. We could call Gray a bridge, or at least a bridge-builder: between the neoclassical values of the Augustan Age and the romantic values of the late eighteenth century, and also between the interest of scholarly learning and the fascination of great popularity.

THOMAS HARDY, 1840–1928

Thomas Hardy was born on June 2, 1840, at Upper Bockhampton in Dorset. After several years as an apprentice in architecture, he began writing fiction and, over a thirty-year period, produced fourteen novels and a number of short stories. Then, from 1898, in another thirty-year career, he produced eight volumes of poetry as well as an epic drama, *The Dynasts*. Hardy is the only English-speaking writer who has any serious claim to superlative distinction in both fiction and poetry. At least five of his novels belong in the first rank: *Far from the Madding Crowd, The Return of the Native, The Mayor of Casterbridge, Tess of the d'Urbervilles,* and *Jude the Obscure.* And successive generations of poets on both sides of the Atlantic, including Ezra Pound, John Crowe Ransom, W. H. Auden, Dylan Thomas, and Philip Larkin, have recognized Hardy's preeminence as a versifier.

GEORGE HERBERT, 1593–1633

The brother of Lord Herbert of Cherbury, George Herbert spent his early maturity as an apprentice courtier, but in his early thirties he took orders and spent the remaining few years of his life (he died at thirty-nine) as a most devout clergyman and as a religious poet of great intellect and passion. His poetry, mostly contained in *The Temple; or, Sacred Poems and Private Ejaculations,* was not published until 1633, after Herbert's death. The book has remained a favorite for three and a half centuries.

ROBERT HERRICK, 1591–1674

Herrick was superficially a good deal like his near-contemporary George Herbert: a poet and clergyman educated at Cambridge. But, markedly unlike the pious and saintly Herbert, Herrick was much better at secular poetry than at the sacred. In his marvelously constructed lyrics, there is an appreciation of nature and the physical — including the body, with and without clothes.

GERARD MANLEY HOPKINS, 1844–1889

Only now, more than a hundred years after his death, is Hopkins receiving the attention that he deserves. He converted to Catholicism while an undergraduate at Oxford and became a Jesuit priest in 1877. He wrote relatively little, and none of his poems were published during his lifetime. The poems were marked by idiosyncrasies — of vocabulary, syntax, and acoustic effects — that set them off from his contemporaries' writings and delayed the appreciation of his verses for many years. Even now we are still learning to catch up with his innovations, which are testimony to the authenticity of Hopkins's enormous feeling — ecstasy in many cases, desperation in a few.

A. E. HOUSMAN, 1859–1936

The book for which Alfred Edward Housman is most famous is called *A Shropshire Lad,* but Housman was not from Shropshire and he was hardly a lad when the book was published in 1896. He was born in Worcestershire, which is near Shropshire, and spent a melancholy and undistinguished time at Oxford before taking a clerical job in the Patent Office in 1882. Eventually, however, he joined the faculty of University College, London, as a teacher of Latin, and later went to Cambridge. He was a distinguished editor and educator. Housman was old-fashioned, patriotic, conservative, and conventional in literature; but he was one of the first people in history to fly commercially.

RANDALL JARRELL, 1914–1965

Jarrell is the youngest American poet in this book, and, with the exception of Dylan Thomas, the youngest of any nationality. He was born in Tennessee and died in North Carolina, but significant parts of his life were spent outside the South—childhood in California, World War II in the Army Air Corps, some teaching time at Kenyon College in Ohio and elsewhere. He was a student, colleague, or friend of John Crowe Ransom and Cleanth Brooks, and he can be grouped as a younger member of the Fugitive-Agrarian group and the New Critics. In writing fiction and criticism as well as poetry, Jarrell resembles his somewhat older contemporary, Robert Penn Warren. Jarrell was a bold and witty critic who could appreciate Walt Whitman, Robert Frost, and William Carlos Williams at a time when such appreciation was somewhat out of fashion. His poetry is marked by strong feeling and accurate observation of the technology of the modern world. Even though we know that people have been dying horribly in war for thousands of years, modern warfare has brought new and deeper horrors, of which Jarrell was peculiarly, eloquently cognizant.

BEN JONSON, 1572–1637

Ben Jonson is the earliest English writer who is routinely called by a nickname, a familiarity that seems justified by Jonson's vigor and good humor. He was a successful playwright, producing both comedies and tragedies; a translator, conversationalist, and critic of great learning and distinction; and a lyric poet whose grace and energy are the equal of his best classical precursors.

JOHN KEATS, 1795–1821

It is probable that John Keats produced more great poetry at an earlier age than any other poet in this book. Critics sometimes play a game that asks, "What would Shakespeare's (or Milton's, or whosever) reputation be if he (or she) had died, like Keats, at twenty-five?" Keats's father, who kept a livery stable, died in a mishap in 1804, and his mother died of consumption in 1810. Keats was apprenticed to a surgeon, moved to London five years later, and was qualified as a "dresser" and subsequently as a surgeon, in accordance with the medical regulations of the day. Keats's first poems were written under the influence of Edmund Spenser, and all of Keats's work shows something of a Spenserian blend of sensuousness and intellectual depth. Keats renders the sights and sounds that we are accustomed to in poetry, but, more than any other, he also attends to the tastes, odors, and tactile qualities. "The Eve of St. Agnes," for example, is a Spenserian romance in design, but many of the details are devoted to registering the exact feeling of bitter cold or exquisite sweetness. Keats was never a formal critic of the sort who writes essays, reviews, and dissertations, but, in his marvelous letters, he displays one of the finest critical intelligences in English literature.

RICHARD LOVELACE, 1618–1658

Lovelace began as gifted, handsome, amiable, and wealthy, but lost everything in supporting the Royalist cause. His most durable poems reflect the circumstances of his turbulent life; he really was in prison (in 1642, for supporting the King), and he really did go to the wars, fighting and being wounded.

CHRISTOPHER MARLOWE, 1564–1593

Christopher Marlowe was born at Canterbury, educated at Cambridge, and murdered at Deptford, presumably in a quarrel over the "reckoning" or bill at a tavern. In the swift blaze of his career, Marlowe produced a half-dozen tragedies, including *Tamburlaine, Faustus, The Jew of Malta,* and *Edward II,* as well as translations from the Latin of Ovid. In an age of unsurpassed greatness in literature, only Shakespeare was greater than Marlowe. Blank verse was introduced into English by the Earl of Surrey a half-century before Marlowe's plays; Marlowe revived the measure and gave it new strength in the form of "Marlowe's mighty line," with persistent exaggeration of rhetoric and image, along with maximal stress on long syllables (as in Marlowe's best-known lines, "Was this the face that launched a thousand ships/ And burnt the topless towers of Ilium?").

ANDREW MARVELL, 1621–1678

Marvell was born in Yorkshire and educated at Cambridge. Like Edmund Waller, he was a Member of Parliament, and a busy political career saw him serving both the court of Charles II and the Cromwellians. Marvell assisted Milton for a time in the Latin Secretaryship to the Council of State. (It is improbable that two poets of such great stature have been employed so prosaically.) Marvell was a celebrated controversialist and satirist as well as a splendid lyric poet.

JOHN MILTON, 1608–1674

Milton is customarily ranked as the second-greatest poet in English, surpassed only by Shakespeare. There have been attacks—most notably by Samuel Johnson in the eighteenth century and by Ezra Pound and T. S. Eliot in the twentieth—but Milton's place seems secure. He was born in London, the son of a scrivener, and educated at Cambridge. Thereafter he spent several years in retirement, studying and preparing himself for great things. In his thirtieth year he traveled on the Continent and met, among many notables, Galileo. For about the middle twenty years of his life, he took on some unpoetic chores as Latin Secretary to Cromwell's Council of State, and it was not until the Restoration that he was free to return to poetry. His sight was failing during his State service, and by 1663 he was totally blind. His greatest work, *Paradise Lost,* was published in 1667, and *Paradise Regained* and *Samson Agonistes* followed four years later.

THOMAS NASHE, 1567–1601

The life of the anti-Puritan satirist Thomas Nashe looks like a proof of Thomas Hobbes's formulation of men's lives in a state of nature: solitary, nasty, brutish, poor, and short. Nashe has an appealing charm and impressive inventiveness, nevertheless, and he managed, in a short and vexed life, to distinguish himself in comic drama, satire, and prose fiction, writing one of the very earliest adventure novels, *The Unfortunate Traveler; or, The Life of Jack Wilton.* Like quite a few of the sixteenth- and seventeenth-century personages in this book, Nashe was imprisoned, doing time for what may have been construed as seditious slander in *The Isle of Dogs,* which has been lost.

WILFRED OWEN, 1893–1918

Owen was killed right at the end of World War I. He was only twenty-five, but he had had time to produce an impressive variety of poems, most of them dealing with war. He was also a notable technical innovator, especially in rhyming. He was born in Shropshire and educated at London University.

EDGAR ALLAN POE, 1809–1849

Poe's life was short; he was evidently an undiagnosed diabetic, on whom alcohol had a terrible effect (although, as one student of his life has remarked, the sad thing is less a matter of Poe's drinking so much as of eating so little). He was born in Boston but, having been orphaned at an early age, raised in Virginia. He tried the Army for a while, but spent most of his adult life as a literary editor and journalist. In a pitifully short career, he managed to make himself famous as a fabulous inventor—a true American Daedalus—so that it can be persuasively argued that Poe, just about singlehandedly, invented the short story, science fiction, detective fiction, the symbolist poem, and the New Criticism. For various reasons, some of which remain mysterious, Poe has enjoyed, all along, a higher reputation in France than in America or England. True, Poe's diction can be lurid and his verbal effects may seem vulgar, but it seems unfair to say—as both Walter Pater and T. S. Eliot suggested—that the full appreciation of Poe can come only to those whose knowledge of English is imperfect. Since Poe was a great inventor and explorer in one of the oldest American traditions, William Carlos Williams called him "a new DeSoto." It is certain that Poe remains the American writer with the farthest-reaching influence: he understood our deepest fears and desires, and his shadow stretches over many literary provinces, from Jules Verne to Vladimir Nabokov to the films of Stanley Kubrick (the secret code letters in *Dr. Strangelove* are P.O.E., after all).

EZRA POUND, 1885–1972

Among Ezra Pound's several achievements—including original poetry and influential criticism—translation from a large number of foreign languages stands very high indeed. It was part of his genius and of his impudence to translate, with impressive fidelity to the spirit if not always the letter of the original, from languages of which his academic knowledge was imperfect. He was a literal as well as a literary globetrotter. He was born in Idaho, educated in Pennsylvania and New York, employed briefly in Indiana, and exiled for many years in England, France, and Italy. In Italy during World War II he made scores of radio broadcasts defending the fascist powers and attacking the Allies, including the United States. He was accused of treason, but the case was never completed because Pound was adjudged insane and unfit for trial. He was held in the prison wing of a federal mental hospital for more than a dozen years but was finally released, too old to threaten anyone. He returned to Italy in 1959 and lived on for thirteen more years, lapsing toward the end into humility and silence after a long life of obstreperous racket, much of it silly, some of it insane, but some of it of matchless brilliance. He formed many literary friendships, and his importance to the twentieth century stems from his own writing and from that which he stimulated his friends to produce; he was a great instigator and a noble advocate. W. B. Yeats and T. S. Eliot, among many others, testified to Pound's insight and generosity.

SIR WALTER RALEGH, 1554(?)–1618

Ralegh, the second-oldest named poet in this book (only Wyatt is earlier), was chiefly known as a military, political, and diplomatic genius, and also as an inspiring adventurer. He wrote history and poetry of a most distinguished order. For all his brilliance and patriotic service, however, James I still ordered his execution, and he was beheaded.

EDWIN ARLINGTON ROBINSON, 1869–1935

Robinson began obscurely, born in Maine and educated at Harvard. His early books were not successful, but for the last twenty years of his life he was among the most honored American poets, receiving three Pulitzer Prizes. The two poems in this book are typical of one of Robinson's strongest sorts of verse: quick, incisive sketches of the blighted lives of those doomed to a small-town existence. Robinson also wrote ambitious philosophical poems and, in his last years, specialized in Arthurian narratives, including *Merlin, Lancelot,* and *Tristram.* After his death, Robinson's reputation suffered something of an eclipse, but many older and younger poets—including Robert Frost, James Dickey, and James Wright—have borne witness to Robinson's continuing power.

THEODORE ROETHKE, 1908–1963

Theodore Roethke was born in Michigan and spent much of his mature life in the Northwest, teaching at the University of Washington. In the barest externals, his career resembles that of Kenneth Rexroth, who was born in Indiana in 1905 and spent much of his mature life in California. Theirs was a generation of true heartland Americans who could start in the Midwest (like Eliot) and (unlike Eliot) keep moving west, seeking the authentic American soil and idiom. In Roethke's poetry, you cannot avoid the vegetable kingdom in many manifestations, from weeds to roses, from germination to fermentation. Roethke came from a long line of foresters and nurserymen, and every time he heard the word "horticulture" he reached for his typewriter, as it were. Roethke's generation came along about twenty years after the great masters of modern poetry (such as Wallace Stevens, William Carlos Williams, Ezra Pound, and T. S. Eliot); and all of them — W. H. Auden and Rexroth as well as Roethke — seem to represent an oasis of consolidation in a luxuriant desert of expansion and experimentation. Roethke, at any rate, certainly took fewer chances than his immediate forebears — fewer, even, than the slightly more remote Hardy and Yeats. Even so, Roethke was a vigorous and faithful inheritor and conservator of the great tradition.

WILLIAM SHAKESPEARE, 1564–1616

In spite of his eminence as the greatest English poet — and perhaps the greatest poet anywhere, ever — we know relatively little about Shakespeare's life. He came from Stratford-upon-Avon, where his father was a prominent citizen, working as butcher, glover, and wool-merchant. When Shakespeare was eighteen he married a somewhat older woman, Anne Hathaway, who gave birth to a daughter six months after the wedding. During the 1590s he worked in the London theater as actor and playwright. He wrote some long poems, including *Venus and Adonis* and *The Rape of Lucrece,* early in his career, and it is probable that the sonnets that make up half of his poems in this book were done during the 1590s. The three dozen plays for which he is most celebrated are grouped as histories or chronicle plays (which Ezra Pound called "the true English *epos*"), comedies, romances, and tragedies. It is customary to speak of his "four great tragedies" (*Hamlet, King Lear, Macbeth,* and *Othello*), but their stature is in many ways rivaled by that of *Romeo and Juliet* and some of the so-called Roman plays, particularly *Julius Caesar, Antony and Cleopatra,* and *Coriolanus.*

PERCY BYSSHE SHELLEY, 1792–1822

Shelley was born into a substantial Sussex family and educated at Eton and Oxford, being expelled from the latter on account of a pamphlet advocating atheism. His life was complex and turbulent, with an early marriage to Harriet Westbrook, whom he subsequently abandoned to take up with Mary, the daughter of William Godwin and his first wife, Mary Wollstonecraft. When Harriet committed suicide in 1816, Shelley and Mary were married (in 1818 she published *Frankenstein, or the Modern Prometheus*). Shelley resembles Coleridge in his high-minded intellect and critical faculty; he resembles his close friend Byron in his love for liberty and his preference of the south of Europe, especially Italy, over the north; and he resembles Keats (on whose death he wrote the great pastoral elegy "Adonais") in the range and depth of his lyrics. Shelley was a great translator as well as a great lyric and dramatic poet. He died by drowning when his yacht *Ariel* foundered in a storm off the Italian coast near Leghorn. His body, which washed ashore after a week, was cremated in the presence of Leigh Hunt and Byron.

SIR JOHN SUCKLING, 1609–1642

Sir John Suckling's father was a knight who served as Secretary of State and Comptroller of the Household under James I. Suckling was born in Middlesex and educated at Cambridge. He was a loyal supporter of Charles I. He fled to the Continent early in the Civil War. He died in Paris, purportedly a suicide.

ALFRED TENNYSON, FIRST BARON TENNYSON, 1809–1892

As the centennial of Tennyson's death approaches, a pretty good case could be made to the effect that it has been a full hundred years since the Poet Laureate and the greatest living English poet were the same person. Arguments, as always, may develop about any of the terms of that case, but it remains true that Tennyson was one of the greatest poets who have held the Laureateship. Tennyson was born in Lincolnshire and educated at Cambridge, where he was one of a bright constellation of promising men. Another member of the group was the brilliant Arthur Hallam, a dear friend whose death in 1833 stimulated Tennyson to write the noble and eloquent elegy *In Memoriam* (published in 1850). Tennyson excelled in the short musical lyric, the dramatic monologue, the long narrative, and certain boldly mixed forms for which we still lack accurate names, such as *The Princess* and *Maud*.

DYLAN THOMAS, 1914–1953

Dylan Thomas was a fully mature poet while still an adolescent and published his first book, *18 Poems,* before his twenty-first birthday. Like T. S. Eliot, Hart Crane, and several other modern poets, Thomas began as an extraordinarily complex writer and, by terrific suffering and discipline, struggled through to achieve a breathtaking clarity and simplicity. He was born in Swansea, Wales, son of a schoolteacher. Skipping college, he worked as a writer from the age of twenty until his death, not yet forty years old, in New York. He excelled in both poetry and prose, and he was by far the greatest reader and performer of the modern poets. His flourishing, around 1950, happened to coincide with the emergence of the long-playing phonograph record, and many who would not otherwise have experienced any poetry were privileged to hear Thomas read aloud, either in person or on record. He was in some ways alien to the austerities of the modernists before him and the postmodernists after, but one would have to be totally deaf and ice-cold not to respond to Thomas's magnificent voice. As his two poems in this anthology attest, Thomas belonged in a great tradition that includes William Blake, John Keats, Thomas Hardy, and William Butler Yeats—poets who sang ecstatically and wisely of birth, love, death, and glory.

HENRY VAUGHAN, 1622–1695

Henry Vaughan and his twin brother Thomas were born in a part of southeast Wales once inhabited by the Silures (hence the geological "Silurian Age," by the way); Henry Vaughan styled himself a "Silurist." He studied both law and medicine, and his poems are uniformly saturated in religious feeling. The passion affected Wordsworth a century after Vaughan's death.

EDMUND WALLER, 1606–1687

A complex man surviving in most complex times, Waller was a politician in the good and bad senses. He was a lawyer and, aged sixteen, Member of Parliament, seeming to support the Parliamentarians but really a Royalist who, when exposed in 1643, displayed treachery, cowardice, and faithlessness. No matter. One lovely love poem shines with a clear light and true voice, and all the doublecrossing and crookedness fall away.

WILLIAM WORDSWORTH, 1770–1850

In his long and eventful life, Wordsworth had more to do with the nature of English poetry than any other poet of the past two centuries. After being raised in Cumberland and educated at Cambridge, he spent some time in France at the height of the Revolution. There, also, he and Annette Vallon became the parents of a daughter, Caroline, but for complex reasons the couple did not marry. A succession of legacies, settlements, and sinecures permitted Wordsworth and his sister Dorothy to live simply without needing to earn a living. They occupied dwellings in Dorset, then in Somerset, near Coleridge, at Grasmere in the Lake Country, and finally—in 1813, after he had married Mary Hutchinson—at Rydal Mount. An on-again-off-again friendship with Coleridge was clearly the most important association of Wordsworth's literary life. The two collaborated on the volume called *Lyrical Ballads, with a Few Other Poems,* containing Coleridge's "The Rime of the Ancient Mariner" and a number of Wordsworth's poems, including the meditative masterpiece, "Tintern Abbey." Wordsworth was much honored in his later years, and from 1843 until his death was Poet Laureate.

SIR THOMAS WYATT, 1503–1542

Wyatt is the earliest of the named poets in this book. He was born into a noble family in Kent, educated at Cambridge, and employed as a courtier and diplomat by Henry VIII. He was thought to have had something to do with Anne Boleyn before her marriage, and he was imprisoned briefly after her downfall, but he soon found his way back into the king's favor. Wyatt was witty, learned, and passionate; in technical terms, he was perhaps the most original and inventive of English poets, since he was the first—or at any rate among the first—to use terza rima, ottava rima, and the sonnet (all imported from Italy) as well as one of the best practitioners of the rhyme royal stanza that had been imported from France somewhat earlier. In friendship and in literary relations, Wyatt is commonly linked with Henry Howard, Earl of Surrey.

WILLIAM BUTLER YEATS, 1865–1939

Since Yeats was interested in the occult, we may aptly consider him a typical Gemini (his birthday was June 13)—split, divided, double. His life was neatly divided into a nineteenth-century half and a twentieth-century half; he was both a dreamy dreamer and a hardheaded practical man of affairs; he was a Theosophist and a Rosicrucian but also a Senator. In some ways he was the most Irish of Irishmen, but his family was Protestant and he never mastered the Irish language. His father, John Butler Yeats, was a celebrated painter, and Yeats himself studied art. He soon turned to literature, however, and produced a succession of lovely works in many modes: romantic lyric, political satire, mythic metamorphosis (transforming one of his great loves, Maud Gonne, into a Helen), verse drama, aesthetic criticism, visionary history, and some of the deepest and most entertaining autobiographical writing of the century. He remained single until his fifties, when he married a young woman named Georgie Hyde Lees, with whom he had a son and a daughter, for both of whom he wrote very engaging prayers. Many readers consider Yeats the greatest English-speaking poet of the twentieth century.

ACKNOWLEDGMENTS

Chatto & Windus. Wilfred Owen: "Anthem for Doomed Youth" from *The Poems of Wilfred Owen*, edited by Jon Stallworthy. Reprinted by permission of the Estate of Wilfred Owen and by permission of Chatto & Windus.

Doubleday. Theodore Roethke: "My Papa's Waltz," copyright 1942 by Hearst Magazines, Inc. From *The Collected Poems of Theodore Roethke* by Theodore Roethke. Used by permission of Doubleday, a division of Bantam, Doubleday, Dell Publishing Group, Inc.

Faber and Faber Ltd. W. H. Auden: "Musée des Beaux Arts" from *Collected Poems* by W. H. Auden. T. S. Eliot: "The Love Song of J. Alfred Prufrock" from *Collected Poems 1909–1962* by T. S. Eliot. Randall Jarrell: "The Death of the Ball Turret Gunner" from *The Complete Poems* by Randall Jarrell. Ezra Pound: "The River-Merchant's Wife: A Letter" and "Hugh Selwyn Mauberly" from *Collected Shorter Poems* by Ezra Pound. Theodore Roethke: "My Papa's Waltz" from *The Collected Poems of Theodore Roethke* by Theodore Roethke. Above selections reprinted by permission of Faber and Faber Ltd.

Farrar, Straus & Giroux, Inc. Randall Jarrell: "The Death of the Ball Turret Gunner" from *The Complete Poems* by Randall Jarrell. Copyright © 1945 and renewal copyright © 1972 by Mrs. Randall Jarrell. Reprinted by permission of Farrar, Straus & Giroux, Inc.

Harcourt Brace Jovanovich. T. S. Eliot. "The Love Song of J. Alfred Prufrock" from *Collected Poems 1909–1962* by T. S. Eliot, copyright 1936 by Harcourt Brace Jovanovich, Inc., copyright 1964, 1963 by T. S. Eliot, reprinted by permission of the publisher.

Harvard University Press. Emily Dickinson: "Because I Could Not Stop for Death," "I Heard a Fly Buzz," and "A Narrow Fellow in the Grass" from *The Poems of Emily Dickinson,* Thomas H. Johnson, editor. Cambridge, Mass.: The Belknap Press of Harvard University Press, copyright 1951, © 1955, 1979, 1983 by the President and Fellows of Harvard College.

David Higham Associates Limited. Dylan Thomas: "Do Not Go Gentle into That Good Night" and "Fern Hill" from *The Poems* published by J. M. Dent. Reprinted by permission of David Higham Associates Limited.

Henry Holt & Company. Robert Frost: "Stopping by Woods on a Snowy Evening" and "Mending Wall" from *The Poetry of Robert Frost,* edited by Edward Connery Lathem. Copyright 1923, 1930, 1939, © 1969 by Holt, Rinehart and Winston,

INDEX OF TITLES AND
FIRST LINES

INDEX OF POETS